W9-CLI-793

Pass the Poetry, Please!

LEE BENNETT HOPKINS

Pass the Poetry, Please!

Revised, Enlarged, and Updated Edition

HARPER & ROW, PUBLISHERS New York

To my Poet-friends
who make it all possible
L.B.H.

Acknowledgments for copyrighted material,
appearing on pages 245 and 246,
constitute an extension of this copyright page.

Pass the Poetry, Please!

Printed in the United States of America. For information address Harper & Row Junior Books, 10 East 53rd Street, New York, N.Y. 10022. Published simultaneously in Canada by Fitzhenry & Whiteside Limited, Toronto.
Designed by Patricia Parcell Watts
Revised, Enlarged, and Updated Edition

Library of Congress Cataloging-in-Publication Data
Hopkins, Lee Bennett.
Pass the poetry, please!

Includes bibliographies and indexes.
[illegible] Poetry—Study and teaching (Elementary)

[illegible] 372.6'4 86-45758

[illegible] bdg.)

[illegible] 4 3 2 1

CONTENTS

PREFACE: ix

PART ONE: 1
"Poetry Is So Many Things . . ."
An Introduction

PART TWO: 21
From Mother Goose to Dr. Seuss—and Beyond
Acquainting Students with Poetry

PART THREE: 139
"Butterflies Can Be in Bellies!"
Sparking Children to Write Poetry

PART FOUR: 167
"The Water's Starting to Bleed!"
A Potpourri of Poetry Ideas

A BRIEF AFTERWORD: 227

APPENDIXES: 231
1. Poetry Reflecting Contemporary Issues 233
2. Poetry in Paperback: A Selected List 237
3. Sources of Educational Materials Cited 240
4. Mother Goose Collections 243

ACKNOWLEDGMENTS: 245

AUTHOR INDEX: 249

TITLE INDEX: 252

INDEX OF POETS, POEMS, AND FIRST LINES APPEARING IN PART TWO: 262

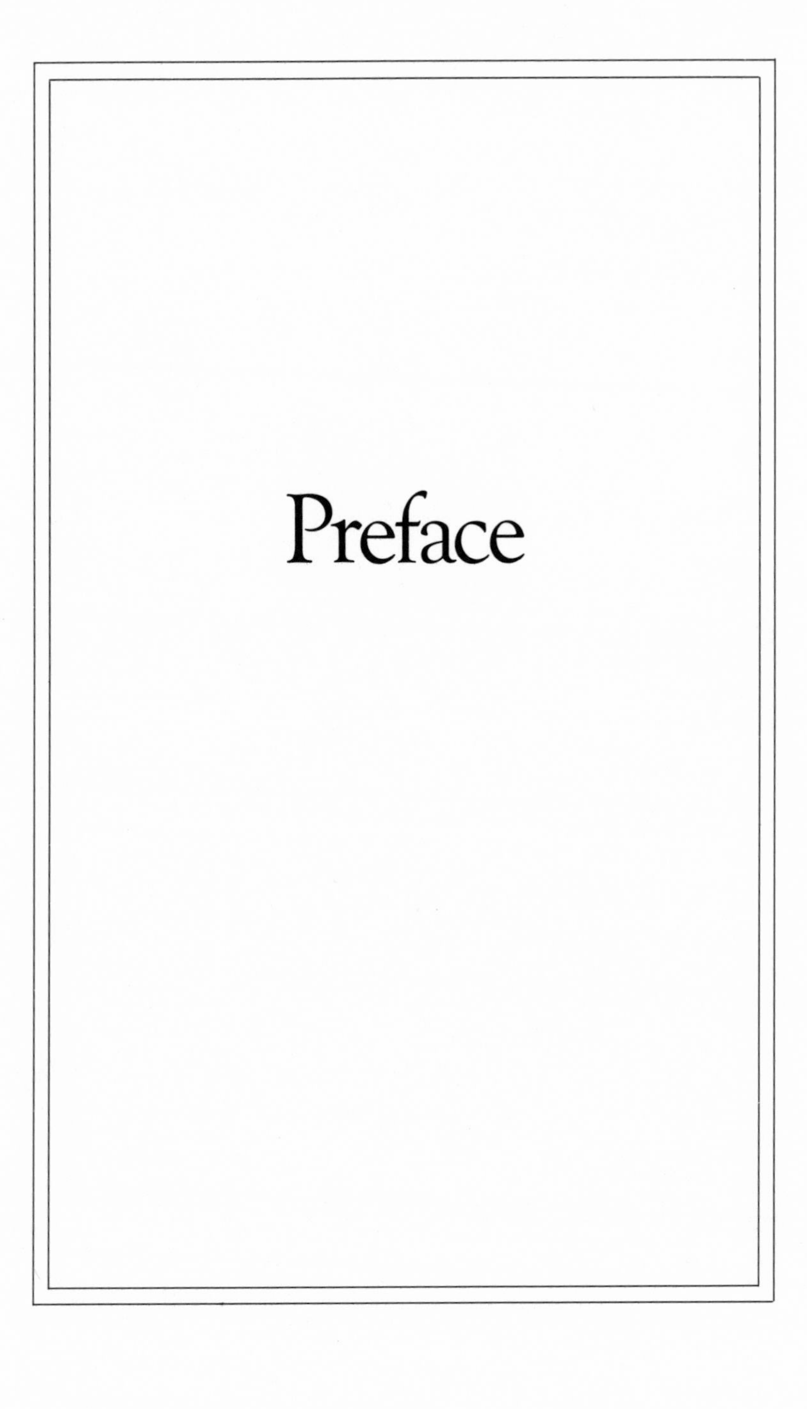

Preface

This totally revised and expanded edition of *Pass the Poetry, Please!* was completed fifteen years after its first publication in 1972. I have reedited, substantially reorganized, enlarged, and updated each of the chapters in terms of important happenings and events that have occurred in the world of poetry for children since the early 1970s.

It has always been my firm belief that poetry can and must be an integral part of the total school curriculum, weaving in and out of every subject area, as well as playing an important part in children's home lives.

References at the end of each chapter give complete bibliographical information—author, title, illustrator, publisher, and copyright data; books available in paperback editions are also noted. "Appendix 3: Sources of Educational Materials Cited," is included to facilitate ordering, and/or for being placed on mailing lists to receive catalogs, book announcements, and other promotional material to keep abreast of newly published volumes.

A great deal of help was offered to make this new edition possible, and I should like to thank the following individuals, to whom I am greatly indebted: Mary L. Allison, who first believed in this project; Misha Arenstein, who listened for long, long hours; Charles John Egita, whose patience never ceased; Teresa Moogan, editor of this revised edition; Margery Tippie, who copiously copyedited the manuscript; the many people in publishing who shared so much, and Marilyn E. Marlow, for being my sage.

Lee Bennett Hopkins
Scarborough, New York

PART ONE

"Poetry Is So Many Things . . ."

An Introduction

An important event in the world of poetry occurred in 1977, when the National Council of Teachers of English (NCTE) established the country's first award for poetry—the NCTE Award for Excellence in Poetry for Children—presented to a poet for his or her aggregate body of work. As of 1982, the award is given every three years. To date, the following poets have received this prestigious honor: David McCord (1977), Aileen Fisher (1978), Karla Kuskin (1979), Myra Cohn Livingston (1980), Eve Merriam (1981), John Ciardi (1982), Lilian Moore (1985). Books by these poets carry the seal pictured below, designed by Karla Kuskin.

New beginnings for poetry for children were also witnessed in the 1980s. For the first time in its history, the John Newbery Medal, an award given annually since 1922 by the American Library Association to the author

of the most distinguished contribution to American literature for children, was presented in 1982 to an original collection of verse—Nancy Willard's *A Visit to William Blake's Inn.* The volume was also named a Caldecott Honor Book for its distinguished illustrations by Alice and Martin Provensen.

Another first for verse came in 1981, when *A Light in the Attic,* by the popular Shel Silverstein, reached number one on *The New York Times Book Review* adult best-seller list. It remained on the list for over three years.

In 1982, T. S. Eliot's *Old Possum's Book of Practical Cats*, upon which the London and Broadway musical productions of the hit show *Cats* is based, reached more readers than it had since it was first published in 1939.

More than ever before, poetry for children has climbed to its proper station. Thank goodness for this trend, for poetry must flow freely in our children's lives; it should come to them as naturally as breathing, for nothing—*no thing*—can ring and rage through hearts and minds as does poetry.

Poetry can work with any grade, any age level. It can meet the interests and abilities of anyone, anywhere, from the gifted to the most reluctant reader; it opens up a world of feelings for children they never thought possible; it is a source of love and hope that children carry with them the rest of their lives.

Children are natural poets. Visit a school playground or park on a spring day and you see youngsters "rhyming." Three children playing jump rope might be exclaiming:

Grace, Grace, dressed in lace
Went upstairs to powder her face.
How many boxes does she use?
One, two, three, four . . .

until one misses, and either this rhyme or another is recited for the next jumper. Another group of children beginning a game of hide-and-go-seek or tag may be deciding who is going to be "it" by chanting:

Eenie, meenie, minee, mo,
Catch a tiger by the toe.
If it hollers, let it go,
Eenie, meenie, minee, mo.

Or:

My mother and your mother were hanging out clothes.
My mother punched your mother right in the nose.
What color blood came out?
R-E-D spells *red* and O-U-T spells *out.*

Still other groups of girls and boys will be bouncing balls, calling out:

A sailing sailor
Went to sea
To see what he could see, see, see.
And all that he could see, see, see
Was the sea, the sea,
The sea, sea, sea.

Children make up their own nonsense rhymes at play, too:

> Booba, booba, baba, baba,
> Twee, twee, toe, toe.
> I know! I know!

Rhyme is very present in the child's world.

For over twenty-five years, during which poetry and I have intertwined in my work as a teacher, consultant, author, and anthologist, I have listened long and hard to girls and boys. My work has taken me across the United States and Canada, and I have encountered thousands of children in a variety of formal and informal situations. Sharing poetry has always been, and always will be, one of the greatest satisfactions of my life. I have seen children in the early grades naturally "ooh" and "ah" when they heard a poem they liked; I have also seen them wince and screw up their faces when a poem did not please them.

In upper grades, poetry has served as an excellent stimulus to better reading and nurtured a love of words. I have used poetry with slow readers in my classes—readers who could not possibly get through a long story or novel but who could understand and relish the message a poem conveys. Poems, being short, are not demanding or frustrating to these readers. They can start them, finish them, and gain from them, without experiencing any discomfort whatsoever.

Many children in the upper grades, whether slow readers or very good readers, may not be mature enough to tackle the sophisticated prose of some of America's men and women of letters, but they can dip into poetry; they can easily read and understand poems by such masters as Carl Sandburg, Robert Frost, Emily Dickinson, and Langston Hughes. Thus, children's literary horizons can be extended through verses created by some of the finest writers.

Children in the elementary grades are not much different from most adults when it comes to knowing and loving poetry. They have their definite tastes just as adults do.

Poetry is so many things to so many people. The anthologist Gerald D. McDonald stated in the preface to his collection *A Way of Knowing* that:

> Poetry can be wittier and funnier than any kind of writing; it can tell us about the world through words we can't forget; it can be tough or it can be tender, it can be fat or lean; it can preach a short sermon or give us a long thought (the shorter the poem sometimes, the longer the thought). And it does all this through the music of words.

The poet David McCord commented to me:

> Poetry is so many things besides the shiver down the spine. It is a new day lying on an unknown doorstep. It is *Peer Gynt* and *Moby-Dick* in a single line. It is the best translation of words that do not exist. It is hot coffee dripping from an icicle. It is the accident involving sudden life. It is the calculus of the imagination. It is the finishing touch to what one could not

finish. It is a hundred things as unexplainable as all our foolish explanations.

A poem is an experience—something that has happened to a person, something that may seem very obvious, an everyday occurrence that has been set down in a minimum number of words and lines as it has never been set down before. These experiences depend upon the poets: who they are, when and where they live, why and how a specific thing affected them at a given moment.

In a eulogy to William Carlos Williams, John Ciardi wrote:

> A good poem celebrates life and quickens us to it. . . . The good poet cannot fail to shame us, for he proves to us instantly that we have never learned to touch, smell, taste, hear, and see. He shames us through our senses by awakening us to a new awareness of the peaks and abysses locked in every commonplace thing. . . . (*Saturday Review*, March 23, 1963, p. 18)

There are as many definitions of poetry as there are poets; their work reflects this diversity, enabling us to choose from a myriad of poems.

Life has produced poets who need the quiet of the country, and they share what their senses reveal. For many the sight of a brook, a reflection in a pond, or "a host of daffodils" inspires fresh images of nature. For others, it is the excitement of the city sidewalks, an image of a fire hydrant, or the city sounds and noises heard that spark verse.

No matter where and when poets live, or where and when they write poetry, all write of everyday happenings from their own points of view about their environments.

Life itself is embodied in poetry, and each poem reveals a bit of life. Good poems make us sigh and say, "Yes, that's just how it is." Or, as Carl Sandburg wrote in his "Tentative (First Models) Definitions of Poetry," thirty-eight gems printed as the preface to *Good Morning, America*: "Poetry is the report of a nuance between two moments when people say, 'Listen!' and 'Did you see it?' 'Did you hear it? What was it?' "

There is really little difference between good poetry for children and good poetry for adults. Poetry for children should appeal to them and meet their emotional needs and interests. We can read about what poetry or a poem *is*, what it *should* do, learn all about meters, rhyme schemes, cadence, and balance; yet all this does not necessarily help to make a poem meaningful. The one criterion we must set for ourselves is that we love the poems we are going to share. If we don't like a particular poem, we shouldn't read it to our children; our distaste will certainly be obvious to them. There are plenty of poems around. Why bother with those that are not pleasing? In the world of poetry almost any theme can be located.

Some people's eyes have flashed at the idea of presenting poetry to children by such greats as E. E. Cummings, Theodore Roethke, or Wallace Stevens, yet it can and has been done successfully. I suppose that once brows were also raised at the thought of bringing "adult literature" into the elementary school or home—books such as *20,000 Leagues Under the Sea* or *Gulliver's Travels.* We know that these novels have proved to be popular with students. The language and thoughts of poetry written primarily for adult audiences can also appeal to girls and boys.

While working with boys and girls across the country, I have always read a balance of the old and new, poems written "for adults," poems written "for children," and often poems written by children for children.

Many classroom teachers and parents may not want to read "sophisticated" poetry to children, particularly if the poetry is somewhat strange to them. Some adults may never feel comfortable reading, to children of primary or even upper-grade ages, such selections as T. S. Eliot's "The Naming of Cats," which I included in the anthology *I Am the Cat*; this poem does have difficult pacing and hard-to-read phrases such as ". . . rapt contemplation" and ". . . ineffable, effable/Effanineffable/Deep and inscrutable singular Name." Many children, however, relish the challenge presented by the richness of Eliot's language.

Karla Kuskin stated:

> There's a line in *The Night Before Christmas* that will stay in my head forever because when I first learned it, I didn't understand all the words.
>
> As dry leaves before the wild hurricane
> fly,

When they meet with an obstacle, mount
to the sky,
So up to the housetop the coursers
they flew,
With a sleigh full of toys,
and St. Nicholas, too.

I didn't know *hurricane*; I didn't know *obstacle*; I didn't know *coursers*; but I just loved the way they sounded.

Because a particular poem works for me, it doesn't mean it will work for everyone. You know your children and their tastes; moreover, you know what appeals to you. Stay comfortable. If "The Naming of Cats" doesn't please you, look for another cat poem. You will find many. In *Index to Poetry for Children and Young People: 1976–1981,* by the anthologists John E. Brewton, George Meredith Blackburn III, and Lorraine A. Blackburn, you can find listed well over one hundred cat poems, and, if dogs are your favorites, you can find over one hundred poems listed about them here, too! Previous volumes in the series, first published in 1942, are also available.

Bringing children and poetry together can be one of the most exciting experiences in parenting or teaching. Over the years, however, I have noted in too many cases what I have coined the DAM approach—dissecting, analyzing, and *meaninglessly* memorizing poetry to death.

Lee Shapiro, a first-year student teacher in one of my graduate classes in children's literature and storytelling at the City College of New York, wrote me:

The children I work with are 2½ to 3 years old. I feel very unsure of what poems I should select for them, which will be appropriate within their capabilities of understanding.

I have felt for a long time that the structured introduction of poetry which I received in public and high school was frustrating and restricting besides being very painful. Being forced to dissect, analyze, and memorize poetry did not leave me much room for enjoyment. Until very recently I have avoided any kind of poetry. Now I have begun to explore on my own with great satisfaction the world of poetry. How much I missed!

I well remember hating Shakespeare as a high school student. I was forced to dissect, analyze, and memorize some fifteen isolated lines from *Julius Caesar.* The class had a written and an oral test on the "Friends, Romans, countrymen . . ." speech. I received an A on the oral but a C on the written test because I misspelled several words and left out some punctuation marks! The next semester I suffered through a similar experience with Alfred Noyes' "The Highwayman." I, too, soon came to detest the sound of the word poetry. It was not something to be enjoyed—it was a test of endurance and memorization ability.

Looking back on those days, I laugh now, but I still wonder why any student has to suffer through poetry presented in such a dreary, uninteresting fashion, as if it were an exercise in total recall. I cannot even remember poems I *myself* wrote and wouldn't attempt reciting them without the printed words in front of me.

As a young teenager, I wanted adventure, mystery,

murder, passion. It wasn't until my adult years that I realized that Shakespeare and poets like Noyes could have given me what I wanted then. Certainly the tragedies of Shakespeare dealt more passionately and romantically with life than did the drugstore magazines I bought with my weekly allowance. But I wasn't aware of this due to my sour poetic experiences.

Eve Merriam comments: "I want children to love poetry, not memorize it."

In his acceptance speech on receiving the 1982 NCTE Excellence in Poetry for Children Award, John Ciardi remarked:

> You can't say, "Memorize . . . and give it back on demand. . . ." You are the ones who must entice the student. If a student can be brought to say, "Wow!" to one poem, he or she can say "Wow!" to another. . . . Unless you and others like you can lead your students to this contact, Pac-Man is going to eat us all.

Unfortunately, there is a steady stream of curriculum guides that advocate dissecting poems to the point of the ridiculous. In one guide, the poem "City" by Langston Hughes is reprinted. The poem, a mere eight lines, beautifully describes a city waking up and going to bed. The guide suggests that after reading the poem aloud to children:

> Ask: What is a city? Name some cities. How does a city spread its wings? What does the poet mean when he says,

"making a song in stone that sings?" How can a city go to bed? How can a city hang lights? Where would a city's head be?

The guide then suggests that children memorize the poem as a group lesson by rote. After this nonsensical interrogation, billed in the guide as an "appreciation lesson," which I doubt any adult would use, it would take a miracle or a child masochist to ever ask for this, or any other poem, again.

In her article "An Unreasonable Excitement," Myra Cohn Livingston comments on the abuse of her poem "Whispers":

> . . . when I find it assaulted in . . . basal readers I want to scream out to well-meaning but misguided educators to cease and desist . . . do not use it to teach about rhyming words or punctuation, do not ask such inane and unanswerable questions as "What does a whisper look like? What color is a whisper?" (*The Advocate,* Spring 1983)

In an article, "A Visit to Robert Frost" by Roger Kahn (*Saturday Evening Post,* November 19, 1980), Frost was asked, "What is the meaning of a poem?" He replied, "What it says." Persisting, the interviewer told Frost, "But we don't know what it means to you." And he answered, "Maybe I don't want you to."

Probably one of the saddest commentaries on the compulsion to analyze in the history of poetry are the endless definitions and interpretations of Robert Frost's most famous, four-stanza, sixteen-line poem, "Stopping by

Woods on a Snowy Evening." Even poet-critics themselves are guilty of endless analysis.

Louis Untermeyer, in *The Pursuit of Poetry,* elaborates on this tearing apart of Mr. Frost's poem and includes the poet's own wry reaction to all this:

> "I've been more bothered with that one than anybody has ever been with any poem in just pressing it with more than it should be pressed for. It means enough without being pressed." Disturbed by "pressers" puzzling about the snowy woods and the miles to go, he said that all the poem means is: "It's all very nice here, but I must be getting home. There are chores to do." At another time when a critic indicated that the last three lines implied that the poet longed for an after-life in heaven, Frost smiled and shook his head. "No, it only means I want to get the hell out of there."

Children, too, "want to get the hell out of there!"

Long before they enter school, long before they can read a printed word, children can be heard chanting familiar Mother Goose rhymes—verses that have come down through centuries. Young children voluntarily reciting Mother Goose melodies do not stop to ponder over the meanings of words unfamiliar to them. They do not know, and may never know, what *curds* or *whey* are; nor do they know or care about the hidden personages behind peculiar names such as Wee Willie Winkie, Little Bo Peep, or the Queen of Hearts. To acquaint very young children with the fact that Mother Goose rhymes were political lampoons or satires about such historical figures as Mary Tudor, Henry VIII, or Mary, Queen of

Scots, would be ludicrous. None of this matters. The children are in love with the easy rhymes, the alliteration, the quick action, and the humor that Mother Goose conveys.

I am often asked, "How do you read a poem aloud to children?" There is no trickery involved in reading poetry aloud. When a poem is read aloud with sincerity, boys and girls will enjoy its rhythm, its music, and will understand the work on their level.

The guidelines below can help those who get butterflies in their stomachs when it comes to presenting poetry. These same points can be shared with children, for they, too, should be reading and sharing poetry aloud.

1. Before reading a poem aloud, read it aloud several times by yourself to get the feel of the words and rhythm. Know the poem well. Mark the words and phrases you would like to emphasize, and then you will read it exactly as you feel it.
2. Follow the rhythm of the poem, reading it naturally. The physical appearance of most poems on the printed page dictates the rhythm and the mood of the words. Some poems are meant to be read softly and slowly; others must be read at a more rapid pace.
3. Make pauses that please you—pauses that make sense. Some poems sound better when the lines are rhythmically strung together. Sometimes great effects can be obtained by pausing at the end of each line. Many of the poems by E. E. Cummings and William Carlos Williams convey greater mood when they are read by pausing at

the end of each short line, as though you were saying something yourself for the first time, thinking of a word or words that will come from your tongue next. Isn't this how we speak? We think as we talk. Sometimes words flow easily—

other times—
they
come
slowly,
thinking-ly
from our
mouths.

4. When reading a poem aloud, speak in a natural voice. Don't change to a high-pitched or bass-pitched tone. Read a poem as though you were telling the children about a new car, or a television program you saw last night. Again, you must be sincere. A poem must interest you as well as be one that you feel is right for your children.

5. After a poem is read, be quiet. Don't feel trapped into asking children questions such as "Did you like it?" Most girls and boys will answer yes—even if they didn't like it—because *you* selected and read it. And what if they didn't like it? By the time you begin finding out the reasons, the poem is destroyed and half of the class will see why they, too, shouldn't like it anymore.

Another reason children may find poetry distasteful is that it is often taught or presented via a one-week, once-a-year unit approach. There are many places within the day where a poem fits snugly. After all, poetry is not the exclusive property of the language arts. Why not open or close your next mathematics lesson with "Arithmetic," a wonderful free-verse selection that can be found in *Rainbows Are Made: Poems by Carl Sandburg*, which I compiled? Or enhance a spelling lesson with David McCord's "You Mustn't Call It Hopsichord," "Spelling Bee," and "The Likes and Looks of Letters," all in *One at a Time*. The unit approach is good for social studies, science, and mathematics—but not for poetry!

We must do all we can to preserve and nurture the love of rhyme, rhythm, and the feeling for words that young children have in them. They hear jingles on television daily; radios, phonographs, and cassette players blare tunes that either parents, peers, or older siblings play incessantly. As they can with Mother Goose rhymes, four-year-olds can sing lyrics to a popular song without *ever* seeing the words in print. They learn the words by repetition and love of a particular word scheme. And ask the average ten-, eleven-, twelve-year-old or teenager how many popular songs he knows! Young people are entranced, almost mesmerized by their personal poets—today's songwriters.

What is poetry? Perhaps the question is best posed in Eleanor Farjeon's verse "Poetry":

> What is Poetry? Who knows?
> Not a rose, but the scent of the rose;
> Not the sky, but the light in the sky;

"Poetry Is So Many Things . . ."

Not the fly, but the gleam of the fly;
Not the sea, but the sound of the sea;
Not myself, but what makes me
See, hear, and feel something that prose
Cannot: and what it is, who knows?

Does it really matter what poetry is? It does matter, however, what it should do, what it should evoke in each and every one of us. Poetry *should* make us "see, hear, and feel something that prose cannot."

What is poetry? What is poetry to *you*? When you find it, when you come across the something that makes you say, "I can *see* it! I can *hear* it! I can *feel* it!"—and when you know that neither *you* nor your *children* may ever seem the same again, you will have found out what poetry truly is.

REFERENCES

Brewton, John E.; Blackburn, George Meredith, III; and Blackburn, Lorraine A. *Index to Poetry for Children and Young People: 1976–1981.* H. W. Wilson Company, 1983.

Eliot, T. S. *Old Possum's Book of Practical Cats.* Illustrated by Edward Gorey. Harcourt Brace Jovanovich, 1982; new edition; also in paperback.

Hopkins, Lee Bennett (selector). *I Am the Cat.* Illustrated by Linda Rochester Richards. Harcourt Brace Jovanovich, 1981.

———. *Rainbows Are Made: Poems by Carl Sandburg.* Illustrated by Fritz Eichenberg. Harcourt Brace Jovanovich, 1982; also in paperback.

McCord, David. *One at a Time: His Collected Poems for the Young.* Illustrated by Henry B. Kane. Little, Brown, 1977.

McDonald, George (compiler). *A Way of Knowing.* Illustrated by Clare and John Ross. T. Y. Crowell, 1959.

Silverstein, Shel. *A Light in the Attic.* Harper & Row, 1981.

Untermeyer, Louis. *The Pursuit of Poetry.* Simon and Schuster, 1969.

Willard, Nancy. *A Visit to William Blake's Inn: Poems for Innocent and Experienced Travelers.* Illustrated by Alice and Martin Provensen. Harcourt Brace Jovanovich, 1981; also in paperback.

PART TWO

From Mother Goose to Dr. Seuss–and Beyond

Acquainting Students with Poets

Perhaps it was the elusive Mother Goose who began poetry for children when she took "Muffet," rhymed it with "tuffet," played around with "thumb" and "plum," and thought up "Hi, diddle, diddle/The cat and the fiddle."

There are many explanations of who the real Mother Goose was. Scholars differ: some claim she was the Queen of Sheba; others say her origin was French, British, or German. The name is *just* a name that originated in Boston, Massachusetts, proclaim many—a moniker that was coined by Thomas Fleet, a well-known Boston printer, whose mother-in-law's name was Elizabeth Vergoose; they say that Fleet printed the very first collection of Mother Goose verses in 1719. Whoever Mother Goose was and wherever the rhymes really originated, they are still an integral ingredient of early childhood and a vital part of world literature.

One of the best reference books on these rhymes of yore is *The Annotated Mother Goose,* edited by William Baring-Gould and Cecil Baring-Gould; this 350-page volume contains rhymes with scholarly explanations and black-and-white illustrations by artists such as Kate Greenaway, Randolph Caldecott, and Walter Crane, along with historical woodcuts. Chapter 1 tells "All About Mother Goose" verses that have become a beloved heritage of "nobody really knows when and where."

Why has Mother Goose had such wide appeal to generation after generation of children? Stop to listen to the rhymes. See how they awaken responsiveness in children. They are short, fun-filled, dramatic, pleasing to the ear, easy to remember—and, oh, so hard to forget.

The step from Mother Goose to other forms of poetry is a small one. Many girls and boys today quickly go from Mother Goose to the nonsense rhymes of Dr. Seuss—a man whose language and characters enchant them. We may never know the true origin of Mother Goose, but we do know that Dr. Seuss is an American, living in La Jolla, California. The doctor, whose real name is Theodor Seuss Geisel, was born in Springfield, Massachusetts, on March 2, 1914. His first book, *And to Think That I Saw It on Mulberry Street*, was immediately acclaimed. Seussian characters, thereafter, have captured the hearts of youngsters and their parents as well. His unforgettable characters—grinches, sneeches, drum-tummied snumms, the Yooks and the Zooks—will probably match Mother Goose's classic characters—pie-men and pumpkin eaters and pretty maids all in a row.

Interviewing Dr. Seuss, I asked, "What is rhyme?" "Rhyme?" he answered. "A rhyme is something without which I would probably be in the dry-cleaning business!" The dry-cleaning business lost a great man, but the world gained from his clever pen.

Many children are raised on Dr. Seuss rhymes. Unfortunately, that is where too many stop, when adults leave them. Children, given guidance, can learn to love poetry written by other contemporary poets, many of whom are discussed within this chapter. Following is a sampling of twenty American poets who have written volumes of original verse and whose works have been widely anthologized. It will serve to introduce the best poetry to boys and girls, motivating them to read the poetry. You can add spice to this information and feed students personal anecdotes about the writers' lives and works.

Throughout this volume I mention titles of many high-quality anthologies; these contain works of both new and older master poets such as A. A. Milne, Walter de la Mare, and others on whom we have all been brought up. It is not my intention to throw away the old, but my desire to bring the new and the now into the lives of children. This leads me to emphasize contemporary poets.

Arnold Adoff

black   is brown   is tan
is girl   is boy
is nose   is face
is all the colors
of the race
is dark   is light
singing songs
in singing night
kiss big woman   hug big man
black   is brown   is tan . . .

—from BLACK IS BROWN IS TAN

Arnold Adoff's first book, *I Am the Darker Brother: An Anthology of Modern Poems by Negro Americans*, grew from his collecting black American poems for use in his own classroom.

"I began collecting literature for my classes while teaching in the late 1950s and early 1960s in Harlem and the Upper West Side of New York City," he told me. "I have been a poet, deep inside, since I began writing as a teenager. By thirty, I was enough of a man to start to put things together and realize where the thrust should be directed. I wanted to influence the kids coming up—not a small group of academic anemics who try to control aspects of the literature of this country. I felt that if I could anthologize adult literature of the highest literary quality and get it into classrooms and libraries for children and young adults, I could make my share of the revolution. I guess when I realized I was too old to learn how to make bombs, I threw myself full-force into creating books for children."

One volume followed another, and Mr. Adoff burst onto the literary scene like a human being thrust from a circus cannon, to produce outstanding volumes of prose, poetry, biography, and picture books.

In 1973, he completed the comprehensive collection *The Poetry of Black America.*

In the late 1970s, he, his wife, Virginia Hamilton, the acclaimed Newbery Award–winning novelist, and their two children, Leigh Hamilton and Jaime Levi, left New York City to settle in Yellow Springs, Ohio. They built a redwood house behind Ms. Hamilton's mother's house.

Defining poetry, Mr. Adoff told me, "There are as many definitions of poetry as there are different kinds of poems, because a fine poem combines the elements of measuring music, with a form like a living frame that holds it all together. My own personal preference is the music first that must sing out to me from the words. How does it sing, sound—then how does it look?

"I look for craft and control in making a form that is unique to the individual poem, that shapes it, holds it tight, creates an inner tension that makes a whole shape out of the words. I really want a poem to sprout roses and spit bullets; this is the ideal combination, and it is a tough tightrope that takes the kind of control that comes only with years of work."

Mr. Adoff was born in the East Bronx section of New York City. "I was a Cancer crab who was born on a hot July Sunday on the fifteenth in 1915. I grew up in and around the Bronx and all over the city and loved New York and its potential for power, excitement and discovery. There was too much to see, always too much to read, always another place to go. The neighborhood had character—a solid, respectable Jewish middle-class, the butcher, the grocer, my father's pharmacy on the corner, the old ladies sitting in the front of the stoops, mothers waiting with jars of milk for the kids' afternoon snacks after school before running to Crotona Park to play ball.

Books and food, recipes and political opinions, Jewish poetry, and whether the dumplings would float on top of the soup were all of equal importance. And reading, of course. I read everything in the house and then all I could carry home each week from the libraries I could reach on Bronx buses."

His work is distinctive, diverse, ranging through titles such as *black is brown is tan*, a picture book about an interracial family; *I Am the Running Girl*, depicting a young girl who describes the joy and pride that running gives her; *Friend Dog*, free verse exploring the relationship between a young girl and her dog; *Eats*, reflecting his passion for food and eating; *All the Colors of the Race*, thirty-six stylistic works, written from the point of view of a child who has a black mother and a white father; *The Cabbages Are Chasing the Rabbits*, in which the hunter becomes the hunted on a day in May; *Tornado!*, powerful verses about the destruction and aftermath of a violent storm; *Under the Early Morning Trees*, telling how a young girl enjoys the closeness of nature; *Sports Pages*, thirty-seven verses dealing with the many moods of sports such as soccer, football, gymnastics, track, and tennis.

Other volumes include *Today We Are Brother and Sister*, *Make a Circle Keep Us In*, *Birds*, and *Big Sister Tells Me That I Am Black.*

The poet can be heard reading his works on two cassettes: *Arnold Adoff Reads Four Complete Books: Eats: Poems, black is brown is tan, OUTside/INside Poems, Birds: Poems*; and *Arnold Adoff Reads Four Complete Books: Eats: Poems, I*

Am the Running Girl, All the Colors of the Race, Johnny Junk Is Dead, both produced by Earworks.

REFERENCES

I Am the Darker Brother: An Anthology of Modern Poems by Negro Americans. Illustrated by Benny Andrews. Macmillan, 1968.

The Poetry of Black America: Anthology of the 20th Century. Harper & Row, 1973.

black is brown is tan. Illustrated by Emily Arnold McCully. Harper & Row, 1973.

Make a Circle Keep Us In. Illustrated by Ronald Himler. Delacorte, 1975.

Big Sister Tells Me That I Am Black. Illustrated by Lorenzo Lynch. Henry Holt, 1976.

Tornado! Poems. Illustrated by Ronald Himler. Dutton, 1977.

Under the Early Morning Trees. Illustrated by Ronald Himler. Dutton, 1978.

Eats: Poems. Illustrated by Susan Russo. Lothrop, Lee & Shepard 1979.

I Am the Running Girl. Illustrated by Ronald Himler. Harper & Row, 1979.

Friend Dog. Illustrated by Troy Howell. J. B. Lippincott, 1980.

Today We Are Brother and Sister. Illustrated by Glo Coalson. Lothrop, Lee & Shepard, 1981.

All the Colors of the Race. Illustrated by John Steptoe. Lothrop, Lee & Shepard, 1982.

Birds: Poems. Illustrated by Troy Howell. J. B. Lippincott, 1982.

The Cabbages Are Chasing the Rabbits. Illustrated by Janet Stevens. Harcourt Brace Jovanovich, 1985.

Sports Pages. Illustrated by Steve Kuzma. J. B. Lippincott, 1986.

Harry Behn

CRICKETS

We cannot say that crickets sing
Since all they do is twang a wing.

Especially when the wind is still
They orchestrate a sunlit hill,

And in the evening blue above
They weave the stars and moon with love,

Then peacefully they chirp all night
Remembering delight, delight . . .

—from CRICKETS AND BULLFROGS
AND WHISPERS OF THUNDER

In an article, "Poetry for Children" (*Horn Book*, April 1966, pp. 163–175), Harry Behn commented on his work:

The poems I shall write about must be mostly my own. They are all I know closely enough. Anything at too great a distance feathers away into a scholarly mist where I am lost and only my intellect can follow, and so all I can do is tell how I happened to write this poem or that—or any at all. I can only guess at what was derived from my own childhood and what I absorbed from my children, and more recently, from theirs.

Mr. Behn was fifty years old before he began writing for children. It began one summer evening when his three-year-old daughter pointed to the stars and said, "Moon-babies." The next day he wrote a poem for her and continued writing poetry until his death in 1973.

Born in McCabe, Arizona, on September 24, 1898, he had the kind of childhood most children today would envy and can only live vicariously via television programs.

"When I was a small boy in Territorial Arizona, in the town of Prescott, in the Bradshaw Mountains, all the boys I played with were influenced by the Native Americans who lived in wickiups on their reservation across Granite Creek. Our parents could still remember massacres or narrow escapes from painted, yelping hostiles and did not love them," he told me.

"The boys were not afraid of the Yavapais. We knew Apaches had been dangerous because they had been treated unfairly. But not even they had been as wicked as gamblers who shot each other once in a while in the bad part of town. . . ."

Upon graduating from high school, he lived one summer with the Blackfeet tribe in Montana, until his parents persuaded him to attend college. In 1922, he received a B.S. degree from Harvard University; the next year he went to Sweden as an American-Scandinavian Fellow; following this he became involved in arts and media, founding and editing *The Arizona Quarterly*, editing anthropological papers, writing movie scenarios, and teaching creative writing at the University of Arizona.

In 1937, he moved to Connecticut to write and travel. He and his wife raised three children.

His first book of poems for children, *The Little Hill*, appeared in 1949, containing thirty poems, many of which have been widely anthologized. Other books include *All Kinds of Time*, an unusual poetic picture book about clocks, time, and the seasons, and *Windy Morning*, a small volume containing many poems about nature and the seasons.

For children in the middle grades, the poet translated Japanese haiku in the volumes *Cricket Songs* and *More Cricket Songs*, with accompanying pictures chosen from the works of Japanese masters.

The Golden Hive, for older readers, reflected his joy in nature, his remembrance of his childhood, and his deep sense of the American past. Undoubtedly, his concerns for nature also stemmed from his childhood years.

He commented, "My earliest memory is of a profound and sunny peace, a change of seasons, spring to summer, summer to fall, and the wonder of being alive. Those are the mysteries I later tried to evoke in poems I wrote about my childhood; the imprints of stillness determining which haiku I chose to translate. . . . Like all aborigines, children are accustomed to thinking about the beginnings of things, the creation of beauty, the wisdom of plants and animals, of how alive everything is, like stars, and wildflowers, and how wonderfully different people can be from each other."

The poet also wrote a book for adults, *Chrysalis: Concerning Children and Poetry*, expressing his views on poetry, as well as several novels for boys and girls.

In 1984, *Crickets and Bullfrogs and Whispers of Thunder: Poems and Pictures by Harry Behn* appeared, for which I culled fifty works from five of his earlier, now out-of-print volumes—*The Little Hill*, *Windy Morning*, *The Wizard in the Well*, *The Golden Hive*, and *Chrysalis*.

In an article, "Profile: Harry Behn" (*Language Arts*, January 1985, pp. 92–94), Peter Roop stated about his work:

Fortunately for us he had the ability to capture a few of life's elusive wonders and cage them on a page. Yet, like everything else that slips away when grasped, we can't squeeze these poems too tightly for they might escape. They are the breath beyond what is.

Harry Behn can be heard reading his own poems on the recording *Poetry Parade*, produced by Weston Woods.

REFERENCES

The Little Hill. Harcourt Brace Jovanovich, 1949.
All Kinds of Time. Harcourt Brace Jovanovich, 1950.
Windy Morning. Harcourt Brace Jovanovich, 1953.
The Wizard in the Well. Harcourt Brace Jovanovich, 1956.
Cricket Songs. Harcourt Brace Jovanovich, 1964.
The Golden Hive. Harcourt Brace Jovanovich, 1966.
Chrysalis: Concerning Children and Poetry. Harcourt Brace Jovanovich, 1968.
More Cricket Songs. Harcourt Brace Jovanovich, 1971.
Crickets and Bullfrogs and Whispers of Thunder. Harcourt Brace Jovanovich, 1984.

N. M. Bodecker

NEW DAY

Mornings bring
both hope
and curses:
God makes
light,
and I make
verses.

—from PIGEON CUBES

N. M. Bodecker was born on January 13, 1922, in Copenhagen, Denmark.

He states, "When I was a child, a one-legged veteran of the last war with Germany, in 1864, still worked his hurdy-gurdy in the country lanes each spring, and patriotic songs remained current in the nursery, reflecting those last sanguinary battles of my grandparents' youth. My conscious childhood spanned the years 1924–33, that sunny upland where so many of my parents' generation thought the world would remain in an age of peace and reason.

"Instead, a new savagery was building, more fearful than the old; and its clouds and foreshadows touched the rims of even the most jealously guarded nursery. What I have retained of my childhood is perhaps more deliberately sunny, more insistently civilized for that reason."

He went to school in 1933, studying at the Birkerød Kostskole, the year Adolf Hitler became German Chancellor. He graduated in 1939, three months before World War II began. Seven months later, Denmark was invaded and occupied by the Germans.

For five years he studied architecture and art at the Copenhagen School of Commerce. Following this he worked as an illustrator and cartoonist on newspapers and magazines, including the well-known *Politiken.*

He lived at his grandparents' home, and because of his

familiarity with the older, Victorian generation, he says that he is "perhaps a late blooming Victorian—at least artistically."

In 1952, he came to the United States to live, working for sixteen years for the "After Hours" department of *Harper's Magazine.* His illustrations have appeared in many major national magazines, including *Saturday Evening Post*, *Esquire*, and *Holiday*, as well as in many major books.

In 1973, *It's Raining Said John Twaining: Danish Nursery Rhymes*, which he translated and illustrated in full color, appeared.

From the nonsense rhymes he had written over a period of years, *Let's Marry Said the Cherry* was published in 1974, with his drawings, followed by *Hurry, Hurry Mary Dear.*

In *A Person from Britain Whose Head Was the Shape of a Mitten*, Mr. Bodecker turned to writing zany limericks. Other volumes include *Pigeon Cubes* and *Snowman Sniffles.*

"My poetry and verse owe their beginning to the gentle, poetic, but indomitable force that was my mother, a joyous, generous woman, positive and clear in all she did. We read together, sang together, made rhymes together; and together we walked through the fields in the evening. There I learned my botany: cornflower, poppy, pimpernel, bindweed and burr, king's candle, plaintain and cinquefoil, names I could no more forget than my own; and on the sandy slope, just before we turned back in the low, eye-blinding sunlight, wildrose, broom, and Lady Mary's shift sleeve—a poetry all its own," he states.

The poet currently lives and works in Hancock, New Hampshire.

REFERENCES

It's Raining Said John Twaining: Danish Nursery Rhymes. Margaret K. McElderry Books/Macmillan, 1973.
Let's Marry Said the Cherry and Other Nonsense Poems. Margaret K. McElderry Books/Macmillan, 1974.
Hurry, Hurry Mary Dear. Margaret K. McElderry Books/Macmillan, 1976.
A Person from Britain Whose Head Was the Shape of a Mitten. Margaret K. McElderry Books/Macmillan, 1980.
Pigeon Cubes and Other Verses. Margaret K. McElderry Books/Macmillan, 1982.
Snowman Sniffles and Other Verses. Margaret K. McElderry Books/Macmillan, 1983.

Gwendolyn Brooks

SKIPPER

I looked in the fish-glass,
And what did I see.
A pale little gold fish
Looked sadly at me.
At the base of the bowl,
So still, he was lying.
"Are you dead, little fish?"
"Oh, no! But I'm dying."
I gave him fresh water
And the best of fish food—
But it was too late.
I did him no good.
I buried him by
Our old garden tree.
Our old garden tree
Will protect him for me.

—from BRONZEVILLE BOYS AND GIRLS

Gwendolyn Brooks is the first black woman to win the Pulitzer Prize for Poetry; it was awarded in 1950, for a volume of her adult poems, *Annie Allen.* Most of the poet's work is directed to mature students and adults.

Ms. Brooks was born in Topeka, Kansas, on June 7, 1917. At an early age she moved to Chicago, Illinois, where she still resides. The state of Illinois named her Poet Laureate, succeeding Carl Sandburg. She is the mother of two grown children, Henry and Nora.

Through her poetry, Ms. Brooks speaks of life's realities in vivid, compassionate words about the black experience.

Fortunately, the poet has written one volume of poems for young readers, *Bronzeville Boys and Girls*, a collection in which she set the task of writing "a poem a day in order to complete the book's deadline." Published in 1956, the book presents poignant views of children living in the crowded conditions of an American inner city. Each of the thirty-four poems bears the name of an individual child and is devoted to his or her thoughts, feelings, and emotions. There is "Val," who does not like the sound "when grownups at parties are laughing," and who would "rather be in the basement," or "rather be outside"; "Keziah," who has a secret place to go; "Paulette," who questions her mother's advice about growing up, posing, "What good is sun if I can't run?"; and "Robert, Who Is a Stranger to Himself."

The first time I read "Skipper" in this slim volume, I recalled my childhood—the day when one of my pet goldfish died. I wasn't terribly upset by its death but was rather taken by my Aunt Doris's advice to "flush it down the toilet." I listened and did what she said. But wouldn't the experience have been richer for me if, instead, I had been given a poem such as "Skipper" to read? Perhaps I, too, like the child in the poem, would have buried my fish beneath a tree. And perhaps I would have come to understand much sooner the value of poetry.

Bronzeville Boys and Girls is one book that should be in every library, available when you want and need it. And you will—time and time again.

Gwendolyn Brooks' life story is chronicled in *Report from Part One*, telling of her family background, childhood years, her " 'prentice years," marriage, children, contacts with other black writers, and her journey to Africa.

In 1962, she was invited by President John F. Kennedy, along with other leading poets, to read some of her poetry at a poetry festival at the Library of Congress in Washington, D.C. There, just prior to his death, she met Robert Frost, who offered warm praises of her work. In 1985 she was named Consultant in Poetry to the Library of Congress for 1985–1986.

On being a poet, she has stated, "I think a little more should be required of the poet than perhaps is required of the sculptor or the painter. The poet deals in words with which everyone is familiar. We all handle words. And I think the poet, if he wants to speak to anyone, is constrained to do something with those words so that they will 'mean something,' will *be* something that a reader may touch."

Now, most of her time is spent writing poetry, lecturing at colleges, and encouraging young poets. She is at work on the second volume of her autobiography plus a book of poems that she writes on scraps of paper "because I want to carry them in my address book. I'm likely to read them at a moment's notice."

REFERENCES

Annie Allen. Harper & Row, 1949.
Bronzeville Boys and Girls. Illustrated by Ronni Solbert. Harper & Row, 1956.
Report from Part One. Broadside Press, 1972.

John Ciardi

MUMMY SLEPT LATE AND DADDY FIXED BREAKFAST

Daddy fixed the breakfast.
He made us each a waffle.
It looked like gravel pudding.
It tasted something awful.

"Ha, ha," he said, "I'll try again.
This time I'll get it right."
But what *I* got was in between
Bituminous and anthracite.

"A little too well done? Oh well,
I'll have to start all over."
That time what landed on my plate
Looked like a manhole cover.

I tried to cut it with a fork:
The fork gave off a spark.
I tried the knife and twisted it
Into a question mark.

I tried it with a hack-saw.
I tried it with a torch.
It didn't even make a dent.
It didn't even scorch.

PASS THE POETRY, PLEASE!

The next time Dad gets breakfast
When Mommy's sleeping late,
I think I'll skip the waffles.
I'd sooner eat the plate!

—from YOU READ TO ME, I'LL READ TO YOU

In an article, "Profile: John Ciardi" (*Language Arts*, November/December 1982, pp. 872–876), Norine Odland, Distinguished Professor of Children's Literature at the University of Minnesota, in Minneapolis, wrote:

> There is magic in the poetry John Ciardi has written for children. He uses words with whimsical agility. Humor in his poems allows a child to reach for new ways to view ordinary things and places in the world. In a few lines, a Ciardi poem can move a listener from one mood to another; the words tell the reader how the poem should be read.

Born in Boston, Massachusetts, on June 24, 1916, the only son of Italian immigrant parents, John Anthony Ciardi grew up in Medford, Massachusetts, where he attended public school. His father, an insurance agent for Metropolitan Life Insurance Company, was killed in an automobile accident in 1919.

Mr. Ciardi began his higher studies at Bates College in Lewiston, Maine, but transferred to Tufts University in Boston, receiving his B.A. degree in 1938. Then, winning a scholarship to the University of Michigan, he obtained his master's degree the next year, and won the first of many awards for his poetry.

"I always wanted to be a poet," he told me. "I took all sorts of courses in English in college and graduate school," he commented. "John Holmes, a fine poet, and my teacher at Tufts, persuaded me to take poetry seriously in my sophomore year. In graduate school, Professor Roy Cowden gave me great help."

One of America's foremost contemporary poets, Mr. Ciardi, a translator of Dante's work, was an English professor at Kansas City University, Harvard, and Rutgers. After twenty years of teaching, he resigned, becoming poetry editor of *Saturday Review* from 1956 to 1972. He had also served as director of the Bread Loaf Writers' Conference at Middlebury College in Vermont, a group he was associated with for almost thirty years.

After successfully writing adult poetry for some time, he decided to write for children because they were around him.

"I wrote first for my sister's children, from about 1947 to 1953, when my wife and I were living with them. Subsequently, I wrote for my own children as they came along, then for myself. My children [John Lyle Pritchard, Myra and Benn Anthony] were in a hurry to grow up; I wasn't, so I wrote for my own childhood."

His own favorite book, *I Met a Man*, a collection of thirty-one poems, appeared in 1961. "It's my favorite because I wrote it on a first-grade vocabulary level when my daughter was in kindergarten. I wanted it to be the first book she read through, and she learned to read from it. Almost any child halfway through first grade should be able to read the first poems. Any bright child toward the end of the first grade should be able to solve the slightly added difficulties of the later poems."

He had no system of writing. "It's like lazy fishing," he once told me. "Drop a line, sit easy. If a fish bites, play it; if not, enjoy the weather!"

He wrote *The Monster Den* about his own children. "It was a way of spoofing them. Kidding with love and some restraint can be a happy relationship. We were never a somber family."

Many of his poems are spoofs of parent-child relationships. "I often write spoofs. I have written some adult poems *about* children that are *not* for them. The closest I come to pointing out the difference between poetry for children versus poetry for adults is that children's poems are *eternal*; adult poems are *mortal*."

Two of his collections, *The Man Who Sang the Sillies* and *You Read to Me, I'll Read to You*, contain such "eternal" verses as "Some Cook!" and "Mummy Slept Late and Daddy Fixed Breakfast." His last collection of children's verse was *Doodle Soup*, thirty-eight mostly humorous verses with such titles as "The Dangers of Taking Baths," "The Best Part of Going Away Is Going Away From You," and "Why Pigs Cannot Write Poems."

His works for children were based on the premise that "poetry and learning are both fun, and children are full of an enormous relish for both. My poetry is just a bubbling up of a natural foolishness, and the idea that maybe you can make language dance a bit. What is poetry? Poetry is where every line comes to rest against a white space. Being a poet is like being a musician. You get caught up in the music. You're drawn to it. So it is with language. It's an instrument and you can't stop playing."

Recipient of the 1982 NCTE Award for Excellence in Poetry for Children, he can be heard on two recordings available from Spoken Arts. On *You Read to Me, I'll Read to You,* he reads to his three children and they read back to him selections from the book of the same title. After an introduction by the poet, thirty-four poems are presented. On side 1 of *You Know Who, John J. Plenty and Fiddler Dan and Other Poems*, he reads twenty-seven poems from the book *You Know Who.* Selections include "Calling All Cowboys" and "What Someone Said When He Was Spanked on the Day Before His Birthday"—true ear-catchers for youngsters. Side 2, geared to older girls and boys, features several longer poems, including "John J. Plenty and Fiddler Dan" and "The King Who Saved Himself from Being Saved."

The poet died on March 30, 1986. Upon his death, John Frederick Nims, retired *Poetry* magazine editor, stated: "I don't know of another poet who so completely put his life into poetry. I don't know of anyone who talked about poetry in a way that made more sense or put things more strikingly . . . he was a very important influence on the poetry of our time."

REFERENCES

I Met a Man. Illustrated by Robert Osborn. Houghton Mifflin, 1961.

The Man Who Sang the Sillies. Illustrated by Edward Gorey. J. B. Lippincott, 1961; also in paperback.

You Read to Me, I'll Read to You. Illustrated by Edward Gorey. J. B. Lippincott, 1962; also in paperback.

You Know Who. Illustrated by Edward Gorey. J. B. Lippincott, 1964.

The Monster Den. Illustrated by Edward Gorey. J. B. Lippincott, 1966.

Doodle Soup. Illustrated by Merle Nacht. Houghton Mifflin, 1985.

Lucille Clifton

5

After a little bit of time
Everett Anderson says, "I knew
my daddy loved me through and through,
and whatever happens when people die,
love doesn't stop, and
neither will I."

—from EVERETT ANDERSON'S GOODBYE

Lucille Clifton was born in Depew, New York, on June 27, 1936. She attended Harvard University and Fredonia State Teacher's College. Her own "roots" are detailed in her eloquent memoir, *Generations*, a eulogy to her parents.

In addition to four volumes of adult poetry, she has created several picture books, including her best known "Everett Anderson" verses. The entire series tenderly portrays black experiences—poems telling about six-year-old Everett Anderson who lives in Apartment 14A. Everett plays in the rain, is afraid of the dark, feels lonely at times, and wonders. In 1970, Everett was "born" in *Some of the Days of Everett Anderson*, which she wrote because she "wanted to write something about a little boy who was like the boys my children might know, for my children and others."

Six additional titles appeared featuring the delightful Everett. In 1983, the last of the series, *Everett Anderson's Goodbye*, gave a touching portrait of the young boy trying to come to grips with his father's death. In a sparse amount of words we follow the child's struggle through the five stages of grief—denial, anger, bargaining, depression, and acceptance.

In an article, "Profile: Lucille Clifton" (*Language Arts*, February 1982, pp. 160–167), Rudine Sims, Professor of Education at Amherst in Massachusetts, interviewed the poet. Therein Mrs. Clifton stated:

I never thought about being a writer. I didn't know it was something you could do. I never heard of Gwen Brooks. The only writers I saw were the portraits they have in school. Like Longfellow. Not even Whitman. They were all bearded men —white, dead, old—and none of that applied to me. It was something that never occurred to me. At first I wrote sonnets and things. You know, you write the kinds of things you read. Then I started writing in a simpler kind of voice, and it didn't seem to me to even be real poetry because it didn't look like the kind of poetry I saw.

In August 1979, Mrs. Clifton was named Poet Laureate of the State of Maryland. Currently, she lives and teaches in California. She has six children—Frederica, Channing, Gillian, Graham, Alexia, and Sidney.

"I had six kids in seven years, and when you have a lot of children you tend to attract children, and you see so many kids, you get ideas from that," she told Rudine Sims.

And I have such a good memory from my own childhood, my own time. I have great respect for young people; I like them enormously.

I didn't read children's books that much because there weren't that many, or if there were I didn't know about them. But my family were great readers, despite the fact that neither graduated from elementary school. Both my parents read books all the time, so I grew up loving books. The love of words was something that was natural to me. My mother even wrote poems. And I grew up reading everything I could get my hands on. I was one of those cereal box readers.

Though Everett Anderson is not part of the household, Mrs. Clifton confessed to me that sometimes she feels he does exist. Occasionally, she has even set a place for him at the dinner table!

At the end of Mrs. Clifton's *Generations*, she writes:

> Things don't fall apart. Things hold. Lines connect in thin ways that last and last and lives become generations made out of pictures and words just kept . . . our lives are more than the days in them, our lives are our line and we go on.

Her lines will continue to go on—and on.

REFERENCES

Some of the Days of Everett Anderson. Illustrated by Evaline Ness. Henry Holt, 1970; also in paperback.
Generations. Random House, 1976.
Everett Anderson's Goodbye. Illustrated by Ann Grifalconi. Henry Holt, 1983.

Beatrice Schenk de Regniers

KEEP A POEM IN YOUR POCKET

Keep a poem in your pocket
and a picture in your head
and you'll never feel lonely
at night when you're in bed.

The little poem will sing to you
the little picture bring to you
a dozen dreams to dance to you
at night when you're in bed.

So—
Keep a picture in your pocket
and a poem in your head
and you'll never feel lonely
at night when you're in bed.

—from SOMETHING SPECIAL

Beatrice Schenk de Regniers' books for children run the gamut from stories about giants to poems about cats and pockets.

"All my books have their own way of working themselves out from me, but most of them begin in a meadow," she told me. "I take my notebook and my pencil and go away, alone, to a place where I can be physically in touch with nature. I wander through the countryside and work in a kind of meadow trance.

"I had a difficult time getting away when I worked on *Something Special*, so I got up every morning at five thirty and worked until seven thirty A.M. The dining room table was my meadow for this book. You know how still everything is between five and seven? The house is so quiet."

Her scenery is her apartment furnishings. She and her husband, Francis, live in a stylish New York City apartment in the West Fifties. Plants and flowers sprout all over; modern paintings adorn the walls, along with works by such well-known illustrators as Irene Haas and Beni Montresor. One has the feeling of visiting a carefully selected museum showing. A large fireplace in the living room adds to the atmosphere of a country place right in the middle of one of New York's most bustling areas.

"I'm in a little house of my own here," she stated, borrowing the idea from her book *A Little House of Your Own*, which is her "autobiography." "I love it here. We're only a block from Central Park [where she rides her bicycle], and we're within walking distance of Lincoln Center. Many summer nights have been spent just sitting at the Center and watching the choreography of the fountains in front of the Metropolitan Opera House."

She has had a lifelong interest in dance. "I love to dance!" she exclaimed. Her face lighted up as if in a spotlight. "In my reincarnation I'm going to be a choreographer. My writing is a kind of dance. I want all my books to have a pace, a movement, like a ballet."

The overture to Mrs. de Regniers' life began on August 16, 1914, in Lafayette, Indiana. At the age of seven, she moved with her parents to Crawfordsville, Indiana, where she lived "a wonderful kind of free childhood, where I could gather violets, live in a tree, walk in the woods—*be!*"

She attended the University of Chicago and Winnetka Graduate Teachers College. She has traveled extensively both on her own and as a welfare officer with the United Nations Relief and Rehabilitation Administration (UNRRA) during World War II. After the war, she served as educational materials director of the American Heart Association. "I got sick of health," she commented, "so I left!"

Her first children's book was *The Giant Story*, illustrated by Maurice Sendak. She knows why she did each book and how they came from within her.

About *May I Bring a Friend?*, illustrated by Beni Montresor, winner of the 1965 Caldecott Medal, she told me, "As gay as *May I Bring a Friend?* is, I wept all the while I was writing it. We had two Siamese–alley cats for ten and eleven years. One of the cats died of cancer; he died in my arms. A year later the other was dying, and I was so distressed I decided to write to focus on something else. The book was done in an almost mechanized way. I said, 'I'll write and not think of cats. I'll write verse because it demands concentration.' I didn't know what I was going to write about, but when the book was finished, oddly enough it was filled with animals—but no cats. Beni and I worked closely together on the book. We would call one another and discuss situations on the phone. I wasn't the least bit surprised that it won the Caldecott Medal. I expect all the illustrators of my books to win it; they are all great." (And three of them have—Maurice Sendak, Beni Montresor, and Nonny Hogrogian.)

Her book *Something Special* is just that. The ten rhymes delight young children. "What Did You Put in Your Pocket?" is a chant; "If We Walked on Our Hands" is gay nonsense about a "mixed up/fixed up/topsey turvey/sit-u-a-tion"; "Little Sounds" gives insight into how wonderful our sense of hearing can be.

Other volumes of her poetry include *It Does Not Say Meow*, nine original verses; *A Bunch of Poems and Verses*; *This Big Cat and Other Cats I've Known*; and *So Many Cats.*

For many years, Mrs. de Regniers was the editor of The Lucky Book Club for Scholastic, Inc.

REFERENCES

The Giant Story. Illustrated by Maurice Sendak. Harper & Row, 1953.

A Little House of Your Own. Illustrated by Irene Haas. Harcourt Brace Jovanovich, 1954.

Something Special. Illustrated by Irene Haas. Harcourt Brace Jovanovich, 1958.

May I Bring a Friend? Illustrated by Beni Montresor. Atheneum, 1964.

It Does Not Say Meow. Illustrated by Paul Galdone. Clarion, 1972; available in paperback.

A Bunch of Poems and Verses. Illustrated by Mary Jane Dunton. Clarion, 1977.

This Big Cat and Other Cats I've Known. Illustrated by Alan Daniel. Crown, 1985.

So Many Cats. Illustrated by Ellen Weiss. Clarion, 1986.

Aileen Fisher

OUT IN THE DARK AND DAYLIGHT

Out in the dark and daylight,
under a cloud or tree,

Out in the park and play light,
out where the wind blows free,

Out in the March or May light,
with shadows and stars to see,

Out in the dark and daylight . . .
that's where I like to be.

—from OUT IN THE DARK
AND DAYLIGHT

Aileen Fisher's first book of poetry, *The Coffee-Pot Face*, was published in 1933. Since that date, she has done numerous original collections as well as longer narrative poems dealing with nature, such as *Listen, Rabbit*; *I Stood Upon a Mountain*; and *Like Nothing at All.*

Since the early 1930s, Aileen Fisher, recipient of the 1978 NCTE Award for Excellence in Poetry for Children, has touched thousands upon thousands of boys and girls with her warm, wise, and wonderful writing.

She was born in, and grew up around, the little town of Iron River, on the Upper Peninsula of Michigan near the Wisconsin border. She told me about her early childhood years.

"I was a lucky child. When I was four years old my father had a serious bout with pneumonia. This made him decide to give up his business in Iron River and more or less retire to the country. He bought forty acres near Iron River and built the big, square, white house where I grew up. We called the place High Banks because it was on a high bank above the river—always red with water pumped from the iron mines. Still, the river was good to wade in, swim in, fish in, and skate on in winter. When I was young, there was still quite a bit of logging nearby, and my brother and I used to follow the iced logging roads. There was a big landing for the logs on the railroad about a mile from our house. We had all kinds of pets—cows, horses, and chickens. And we had a big garden each summer. I loved it. I have always loved the country.

"On my eighth birthday a sister was born. I took immediate charge of her because she was, after all, *my* birthday present. Six years later, another sister came along, but by that time my brother and I were almost ready to go to college.

"I went to the University of Chicago for two years, then transferred to the School of Journalism at the University of Missouri. After receiving my degree in 1927, I worked in a little theater during the summer, then went back to Chicago to look for a job. I found one—as an assistant in a placement bureau for women journalists! That fall, I sold my first poem to *Child Life* magazine, a nine-lined verse entitled 'Otherwise.' "

Ms. Fisher commented on the development of the poem, one that remains among her most frequently reprinted works.

"My aim in Chicago was to save every single cent I was able to so I could escape back to the country life I loved and missed. I had to be economical, so I took a cheap, dark, first-floor room in a third-rate hotel on Chicago's South Side. It had only one window, and that opened onto a cement area that led to an alley. Across the panes were bars to keep prowlers away!

"The room was furnished with a steel cot, a wardrobe badly in need of varnish, two chairs, a kitchen table I used as a desk.

"Coming in from work one evening I jotted down some lines I had thought about on the walk from the station. I then went out to dinner at a small, nearby restaurant where I could get a meal for sixty cents. When I got back to my room I liked the nine lines I hurriedly wrote and sent them off, along with several other verses, to Marjorie Burrows, then editor of *Child Life.*

"I always liked to write verse. My mother had quite a flair for versifying, and I was sort of brought up on it. Mother was an ex-kindergarten teacher, which was fortunate for her offspring."

Ms. Fisher continued writing poems for children, and for five years continued working in Chicago, wondering every day how she might get back to the country. In 1932, she adamantly decided to get out of the city and settled in Colorado. The following year her first book was published, *The Coffee-Pot Face*, a collection of verses, about half of which had previously been published in *Child Life.* The volume was selected as a Junior Literary Guild selection.

Ms. Fisher describes her work habits as always being quite methodical.

"I try to be at my desk four hours a day, from eight A.M. to noon. Ideas come to me out of experience and from reading and remembering. I usually do a first draft by hand. I can't imagine writing verse on a typewriter, and for years I wrote nothing but verse so I formed the habit of thinking with a pencil or pen in hand. I usually rework my material, sometimes more, sometimes less. I never try out my ideas on children, except on the child I used to know—me! Fortunately, I remember pretty well what I used to like to read, think about, and do. I find even today that if I write something I like, children are pretty apt to like it, too. I guess what it amounts to is I never grew up."

Ms. Fisher is tall, solidly built, and "decidedly a country person, addicted to jeans and slacks." Currently, she lives in Boulder, Colorado, at the foot of Flagstaff Mountain.

"My house is well back from the street; skunks and raccoons live nearby, and one year I even found a baby porcupine in my yard. In the winter, deer come right down into this end of town, and I often see groups of them on the side of Flagstaff. I must say city living could be a lot worse! But, of course, I can never forget those wonderful years on the ranch when we lived without electricity, central heating, and automatic water. The wood I chopped, the coal I carried, the ashes I took out! I am afraid I am becoming one of those city softies, but those are all pleasant memories, and I'd do it all over again if I had the chance to."

The ranch she refers to is two hundred acres about a twenty-minute drive from Boulder. She designed and built the house with the help of a friend.

"When we moved to the ranch in 1937, no electricity was available, so we organized our lives very happily without it. When we could finally have it, we didn't want it!

"I'm not or ever was a bit gadget-minded. My favorite possessions are books, and interesting pieces of Colorado wood from the timberline, which have been enhanced by wood rasp, chisel, and some sandpaper.

"My pleasures in life are found through animals, especially dogs, mountain climbing, hiking, working with wood, unorthodox gardening, a few people in small doses, and *reading.* I like centrality in my life and peace and quiet, which means that I avoid commercialized excitement, cities, traffic, polluted air, noise, confusion, travel, crowds, and airports. For me early morning on a mountain trail is the height of bliss."

Recently, with a partner, she ventured into real estate, buying a few old houses and restoring them. "It's been fun," she said. "I am sure I was a carpenter in my last incarnation."

Like many authors, Ms. Fisher receives much fan mail, revealing that boys and girls want to know details about everything, "especially pets, weather, electricity, mountains, and cabins."

Regarding poetry, her first love, she stated, "Poetry is a rhythmical piece of writing that leaves the reader feeling that life is a little richer than before, a little more full of wonder, beauty, or just plain delight."

A *must* for classrooms is her bounty of 140 poems, *Out in the Dark and Daylight*, reflecting various moods of the four seasons. Recent titles include *Rabbits, Rabbits* and *When It Comes to Bugs.*

She can be heard reading thirty-one of her poems on the recording *Poetry Parade* (Weston Woods).

REFERENCES

The Coffee-Pot Face. McBride Company, 1933.

Listen, Rabbit. Illustrated by Symeon Shimin. T. Y. Crowell, 1964.

Like Nothing at All. Illustrated by Leonard Weisgard. T. Y. Crowell, 1969.

I Stood Upon a Mountain. Illustrated by Blair Lent. T. Y. Crowell, 1979.

Out in the Dark and Daylight. Illustrated by Gail Owens. Harper & Row, 1980.

Rabbits, Rabbits. Illustrated by Gail Niemann. Harper & Row, 1983.

When It Comes to Bugs. Illustrated by Chris and Bruce Degen. Harper & Row, 1986.

Robert Frost

THE PASTURE

I'm going out to clean the pasture spring;
I'll only stop to rake the leaves away
(And wait to watch the water clear, I may):
I sha'n't be gone long. —You come too.

I'm going out to fetch the little calf
That's standing by the mother. It's so young
It totters when she licks it with her tongue.
I sha'n't be gone long. —You come too.

—from THE POETRY OF ROBERT FROST

Robert Lee Frost, born in San Francisco, California, on March 26, 1874, did not attend school until he was about twelve years old, and never read a book until he was fourteen.

In *Interviews with Robert Frost*, by Edwin Connery Lathem, a Frost scholar and friend of the poet, the subject commented, ". . . after I had read my first book a new world opened up for me, and after that I devoured as many of them as I could lay my hands on. But by the time I was fifteen, I was already beginning to write verses."

In 1885, after his father's death, he moved with his mother and sister to Lawrence, Massachusetts, his father's birthplace, where in 1890 his first poem, "La Noche Triste," was published in the school paper. Upon graduation from Lawrence High School, he was co-valedictorian. The other student to win this honor was Eleanor White, who became his wife in 1895.

Mr. Frost attended Dartmouth College, but left before taking term examinations to teach in his mother's private school. From 1897 to 1899 he attended Harvard University but left due to illness. After this, as he vacillated between teaching and dairy farming, he grew as a poet.

In 1912, Mr. Frost, with his wife and four children, moved to England, where his first book, *A Boy's Will*, appeared—a collection of thirty poems written between 1892 and 1912. The following year, *North of Boston*, which included his epic work "The Death of the Hired

Man," was published. Mr. Frost, at age forty, had now earned approximately $200.00 from his poetry!

When World War I broke out in 1914, he moved his family back to the United States. Here, at Grand Central Station in New York City, he noticed the *New Republic* magazine; his name and the title "The Death of the Hired Man" were on the cover. He soon found out that Henry Holt and Company was publishing his poetry in the United States; he remained with them for his entire career.

During his lifetime, honor upon honor was bestowed upon him; he was the only person ever to win four Pulitzer Prizes. His own family life, however, was filled with personal tragedies. His sister, Jeanie, became mentally ill and was institutionalized; one daughter, Marjorie, died in childbirth, a year after her marriage; his only son, Carol, committed suicide; another daughter, Irma, was hospitalized as an invalid.

An invitation to participate in the inauguration of President John F. Kennedy was a milestone in his career. Television viewers across the country witnessed an unforgettable incident on this day, January 20, 1961. When the sun's glare and some gusty wind prevented the poet from reading "The Gift Outright," published almost twenty years before the occasion in *The Witness Tree*, he put the sheet of paper in his overcoat pocket and recited the verse from memory.

On March 26, 1962, on his eighty-eighth birthday, Mr. Frost was awarded the Congressional Medal at the White House by President Kennedy. His last book, *In the Clearing*, was published that same year.

He died on January 29, 1963. Upon his death, President Kennedy said, "His death impoverishes us all; but he has bequeathed his nation a body of imperishable verse from which Americans will forever gain joy and understanding."

A biography for mature readers is *A Restless Spirit*, by Natalie S. Bober, which chronicles the poet's life and work.

For adult readers, *Frost: A Literary Life Recommended*, by William H. Pritchard, offers a biography with keen insights into the creative process of the poet and his work.

Robert Frost's poems selected for children appear in *You Come Too*, a collection of fifty-one poems, and in *A Swinger of Birches*, thirty-eight selections, also available on a cassette read by Clifton Fadiman.

In 1978, Susan Jeffers published the first picture-book version of "Stopping by Woods on a Snowy Evening"—a volume to share with all ages.

Robert Frost can be heard on two recordings: *Robert Frost in Recital*, featuring twenty-six selections preserved by The Poetry Center of the 92nd Street YM/YWHA in New York City, which recorded Mr. Frost during three readings given in 1953 and 1954; and *Robert Frost Reads "The Road Not Taken" and Other Poems*, made in his home in Cambridge, Massachusetts, in 1956, containing twenty-three selections. Both recordings are available from Caedmon.

Also available is a twenty-two-minute film, *Robert Frost's New England*, which has garnered a host of media awards, produced by Churchill Films.

REFERENCES

A Boy's Will. David Nutt, 1913.

North of Boston. David Nutt, 1914.

The Witness Tree. Henry Holt, 1942.

You Come Too: Favorite Poems for Young Readers. Illustrated by Thomas W. Nason. Henry Holt, 1959.

In the Clearing. Henry Holt, 1962.

Stopping by Woods on a Snowy Evening. Illustrated by Susan Jeffers. Dutton, 1978.

A Swinger of Birches: Poetry of Robert Frost for Young People. Illustrated by Peter Koeppen. Stemmer House, 1982; also in paperback.

Bober, Natalie S. *A Restless Spirit: The Story of Robert Frost.* Atheneum, 1981.

Lathem, Edward Connery. *Interviews with Robert Frost.* Henry Holt, 1966.

——— (editor). *The Poetry of Robert Frost: The Collected Poems, Complete and Unabridged.* Henry Holt, 1969; also in paperback.

Pritchard, William H. *Frost: A Literary Life Recommended.* Oxford University Press, 1985; paperback.

Nikki Giovanni

WINTER

Frogs burrow the mud
snails bury themselves
and I air my quilts
preparing for the cold

Dogs grow more hair
mothers make oatmeal
and little boys and girls
take Father John's Medicine

Bears store fat
chipmunks gather nuts
and I collect books
For the coming winter

—from COTTON CANDY
ON A RAINY DAY

Nikki Giovanni, born on June 7, 1943, in Knoxville, Tennessee, named after her mother, Yolande Corneila Giovanni, was two months old when her family moved to Cincinnati, Ohio, where she currently lives—"sometimes!" She states, "I have one room in New York, three rooms in Cincinnati, and toilet privileges in Seattle, Washington."

At the age of sixteen, she entered Fisk University in Nashville, Tennessee, majoring in history, but did not graduate until eight years later. Upon graduation she did additional graduate work at several schools.

Ms. Giovanni became an assistant professor of English at Rutgers University in New Jersey. She has also held positions as an editorial consultant and columnist for *Encore*, *American*, and *Worldwide News Magazine.*

Her first book of adult poems, *Black Judgement*, was published in 1968 by Broadside Press. Indeed a broadside, this slim, thirty-six-page paperback introduced thirty-six poems. A steady stream of titles followed, each reflecting her deep involvement in the black experience.

Her first book of poetry for children was *Spin a Soft Black Song*, verses resulting from her volunteer activities for the Reading Is Fundamental program. A revised edition of the volume was published in 1985, with new illustrations and a new introduction.

Ego-Tripping, published in 1973, contains selected earlier works, with the addition of several new poems written especially for the volume; two of her widely anthologized biographical poems, "Nikki-Rosa" and "Knoxville, Tennessee," first published in *Black Judgement*, are included.

Vacation Time, her third book for children, appeared in 1980, containing twenty-two new verses.

"My basic philosophy about writing for children—or any other group—is that the reader is both interested and intelligent," she states. "As a lover of children's literature, I always enjoyed a good story, whether happy or sad. I think poetry, when it is most effective, tells of capturing a moment, and I make it the best I can because it's going to live.

"When I think of poems most children read, from Robert Louis Stevenson to some of the modern poets, I think of an idea being conveyed. The image is important but the idea is the heart."

A collection of autobiographical essays, *Gemini*, published in 1971, was a nominee for the National Book Award. The volume explores her own life and times with the fierce intensity of a poet and lover of life.

Nineteen seventy-eight marked her tenth year as a published author with her adult collection *Cotton Candy on a Rainy Day.* The front dust-cover flap sums up a lot of her life and philosophy:

> She is a widget, a ball bearing, a tiny drop of oil, a very practical person who does what she does because that's all she can do.
>
> She is a storyteller, believing the function of art is to com-

municate; a poet hoping that poems will help soothe the loneliness and fear that life itself brings.

Nikki Giovanni is *Cotton Candy on a Rainy Day.* She thinks we all are.

She has twice been among the top ten American women of influence and holds many honorary doctorate degrees and keys to many cities. When President Jimmy Carter invited the poet to join the President's Committee on the International Year of the Child, she replied, "As a former child, I accept."

The poet loves music and travel, especially to remote places away from television and the telephone. She is the mother of a grown son, Tommy.

At the end of *Gemini*, she writes:

> I think we are all capable of tremendous beauty once we decide we are beautiful or of giving a lot of love once we understand love is possible, and of making the world over in that image should we choose to. I really like to think a Black, beautiful loving world is possible. I really do, I think.

The poet can be heard reading selected works for children on the recording *The Reason I Like Chocolate* (Folkways).

On the filmstrip set *First Choice: Poets and Poetry* (Pied Piper), she is seen strolling the streets of New York City, showing youngsters how the colors, sounds, and rhythms of sidewalk musicians, vendors, and children's games can be turned into verse.

In part 2 of the filmstrip, a workshop lesson, she shows

how students can make discoveries for themselves, including sensory descriptions to create a poem about rain or a picnic. Included are a teacher's guide, brief biographical information, and nine poems reprinted from her various works.

REFERENCES

Black Judgement. Broadside Press, 1968.

Gemini: An Extended Autobiographical Statement on My First Twenty-Five Years of Being a Black Poet. Bobbs-Merrill, 1971.

Ego-Tripping and Other Poems for Young People. Illustrated by George Ford. Lawrence Hill, 1973.

Cotton Candy on a Rainy Day. William Morrow, 1978.

Vacation Time. Illustrated by Marisabina Russo. William Morrow, 1980.

Spin a Soft Black Song. Illustrated by George Martins. Hill and Wang, revised edition, 1985.

Langston Hughes

DREAMS

Hold fast to dreams
For if dreams die
Life is a broken-winged bird
That cannot fly.

Hold fast to dreams
For when dreams go
Life is a barren field
Frozen with snow.

—from SELECTED POEMS

Langston Hughes, a multitalented personality, wrote nonfiction books for children, novels, short stories, plays, operas, operettas, newspaper columns, and a wide variety of poetry.

Mr. Hughes was born on February 1, 1902, in Joplin, Missouri. His childhood was spent shifting from one place to another, from relative to relative. His father, James Hughes, had studied law but because he was black he was refused the right to take his bar examination. Angry and fed up with Jim Crow society, he walked out of the house one day and went to Mexico. Like his father, Langston Hughes endured much racial discrimination.

He attended Central High School in Cleveland, Ohio, where an English teacher, Miss Ethel Weimer, introduced him to the work of poets, among them Carl Sandburg and Robert Frost. In his senior year, he was elected editor of the yearbook and class poet because of his contributions of poems to the school newspaper.

Mr. Hughes went to visit his father upon graduation. On a train heading south for Mexico, he wrote "The Negro Speaks of Rivers," a poem that has become one of his best-known compositions. Later, he sent the poem to Dr. W.E.B. DuBois, an early proponent of black rights, then editor of *The Crisis* magazine, a journal that spoke for an organization that had been recently founded, the National Association for the Advancement of Colored People (NAACP). Printed in *The Crisis*, it was Mr. Hughes' first poem to appear in a magazine for adult readers. The following month, "Aunt Sue's Stories" was published in *The Crisis.* The poem was written about his grandmother, with whom he had lived. She died when he was twelve years old. Mr. Hughes was soon to become known as the Black Poet Laureate, his work appearing frequently in *The Crisis.*

He began a series of wanderings, in manhood, across the world—in parts of Europe, Russia, and Africa. While traveling he worked at a potpourri of jobs, from dishwashing in a Parisian cafe to ranching on his father's Mexican ranch.

His first book of poetry, *The Weary Blues*, was published in 1926 by Alfred A. Knopf. From this date on his works regularly appeared in print, including stories about an important creation, Jesse B. Semple, later known as Simple, a philosophical character with problems typical of those faced by blacks.

Mr. Hughes completed his college education in 1929, graduating from Lincoln University, in Pennsylvania, a college for black men. Later, he moved to Harlem in New York City, where he lived until his death on May 22, 1967.

Four excellent biographies that provide additional background information include a simply written volume for younger readers, *Langston Hughes*, by Alice Walker; *Langston Hughes*, by Elisabeth P. Myers, offering an introduction to the man and his work geared to middle-grade readers; *Langston Hughes*, by Milton Meltzer; and *Langston: A Play*, by Ossie Davis.

Mr. Meltzer, a friend of Mr. Hughes', collaborated with him on two histories: *A Picture History of the Negro in America* and *Black Magic: A Pictorial History of the Negro in American Entertainment*. Mr. Meltzer's biography of the poet was a runner-up for the 1969 National Book Award.

Ossie Davis, a distinguished actor/playwright, was influenced by Mr. Hughes' poems when he first encountered them as a high school student in Waycross, Georgia. He and his wife, actress Ruby Dee, became friends of Mr. Hughes' in the years after World War II when the poet lived in Harlem. Mr. Davis' play about Mr. Hughes is set in the early 1900s, with a cast of nine characters. Excerpts from Mr. Hughes' poems are interwoven with the dialogue.

Three additional adult references are *Arna Bontemps/Langston Hughes—Letters, 1925–1967*, selected and edited by Charles H. Nichols; *Langston Hughes: Before and Beyond Harlem*, by Faith Berry; and *The Life of Langston Hughes: I, Too, Sing America* by Arnold Rampersad.

Folkways has produced a classic recording, *The Dream Keeper and Other Poems*, featuring Langston Hughes reading selections for young people from the book of the same title. Mr. Hughes shows how his poetry developed from specific experiences and ideas in a warm, witty narrative: A trip to the waterfront inspired "Waterfront Streets"; from an old woman's memory of slavery, he created "Aunt Sue's Stories"; an idea that people should treasure their dreams became his famous poem "Dreams." The narrative by this master poet leads naturally into each of his selections; the script is biographical.

Caedmon has produced *The Poetry of Langston Hughes*, featuring fifty poems read by Ruby Dee and Ossie Davis. This recording, for mature listeners, includes four of the poet's "Madam" poems; his tribute, "Frederick Douglass: 1817–1895"; and "Juke Box Love Song." He can also be heard on *Poetry and Reflections* (also Caedmon), which includes nineteen verses with program notes by Ossie Davis.

The poet's work is widely anthologized. In his poetry he spoke of the elements and emotions of life—love, hate, aspirations, despair; he wrote in the language of today, and he does, and always will, speak for tomorrow.

While traveling around the country as a consultant to Bank Street College of Education, I had the opportunity to read his works to students of various ages and backgrounds. Two years after the poet's death, I selected poems that I had found most meaningful to children. The result became the collection *Don't You Turn Back.* Divided into four sections—"My People," "Prayers and Dreams," "Out to Sea," and "I, Too, Am a Negro"—the works represent a wide range of Mr. Hughes' life experiences, from his first published poem, "The Negro Speaks of Rivers," to "Color," which appeared in *The Panther and the Lash,* published after the poet's death.

Many eulogies have been written about the poet and his contributions to American literature. Perhaps the most tender was one created by a fourth-grade Harlem girl who knew and loved his work. She wrote this poem the day after Mr. Hughes died:

IN MEMORIAM TO LANGSTON HUGHES

THE USELESS PEN

A pen lay useless on the desk.
A mother once held a babe on her breast.
Where is the lad this very day?
Down by Poetry Bay they say,
Where the Poets sit and think all day
Of a way to make people happy.
Even though they are not here today
I know they meet by Poetry Bay
Trying to think of a special way
To welcome Langston to Poetry Bay.

REFERENCES

The Weary Blues. Alfred A. Knopf, 1926.

The Dream Keeper and Other Poems. Illustrated by Helen Sewall. Alfred A. Knopf, 1932; reissue 1986.

Selected Poems. Alfred A. Knopf, 1959.

The Panther and the Lash. Alfred A. Knopf, 1967.

Berry, Faith. *Langston Hughes: Before and Beyond Harlem.* Lawrence Hill, 1983; also in paperback.

Davis, Ossie. *Langston: A Play.* Delacorte, 1982.

Hopkins, Lee Bennett (selector). *Don't You Turn Back: Poems by Langston Hughes.* Illustrated by Ann Grifalconi. Alfred A. Knopf, 1969.

Hughes, Langston, and Milton Meltzer. *Black Magic: A Pictorial History of the Negro in American Entertainment.* Prentice-Hall, 1967.

———. *A Picture History of the Negro in America.* Crown, 1956, 1963.

Meltzer, Milton. *Langston Hughes: A Biography.* T. Y. Crowell, 1968.

Myers, Elisabeth P. *Langston Hughes: Poet of His People.* Illustrated by Russell Hoover. Garrard, 1970; Dell paperback.

Nichols, Charles A. *Arna Bontemps/Langston Hughes—Letters, 1925–1967.* Dodd, Mead, 1980.

Rampersad, Arnold. *The Life of Langston Hughes: I, Too, Sing America.* Oxford University Press, 1986.

Walker, Alice. *Langston Hughes: American Poet.* Illustrated by Don Miller. T. Y. Crowell, 1974.

X. J. Kennedy

BLOW-UP

Our cherry tree
Unfolds whole loads
Of pink-white bloom—
It just explodes.

For three short days
Its petals last.
Oh, what a waste.
But what a blast.

—from THE FORGETFUL
WISHING WELL

X. J. Kennedy has been preoccupied with writing since the age of nine or ten. In seventh grade he published homemade comic books on a gelatin-pan duplicator and peddled them for nickels to friends; he also became the editor-in-chief of a woman's magazine with a circulation of one—his mother!

"After college," he states, "I determined on a career as a writer for science fiction magazines, but at the end of six months had sold only two fifty-dollar stories, and so ignobly abandoned the field to Isaac Asimov. After a hitch in the Navy, then a year in Paris studying French irregular verbs on the G.I. Bill, I stumbled into college teaching and eventually became an English professor at Tufts, near Boston, Massachusetts. In 1977, I left teaching to write for a living, and have been doing so happily ever since."

His first adult book, *Nude Descending from a Staircase*, was published in 1961, followed by two more collections, and a volume of selected poems, published in England.

Until 1975, he was best known as a poet who wrote for adults. He also wrote, and continues to write, textbooks and nonfiction, including *An Introduction to Poetry*, which has been used by hundreds of thousands of college students.

For years he wrote verses for children but did little with them. One day, in the 1970s, he received a letter from Myra Cohn Livingston, who liked some of his verses from *Nude Descending from a Staircase*, and wanted to know if he had written verse for children. Via Mrs. Livingston, Margaret K. McElderry, the reknowned editor at Macmillan, heard about him and invited him to do a manuscript of verses for children. The result was *One Winter Night in August and Other Nonsense Jingles*, a rollicking collection of over fifty selections. In 1979, he created *The Phantom Ice Cream Man.*

Nineteen eighty-two marked the publication of *Did Adam Name the Vinegarroon?*, twenty-six alphabet rhymes about mythological and real beasts, featuring such creatures as "Archeopteryx," "Crocodile," "Electric Eel," and "Minotaur." Recent volumes for older readers include *Brats*, forty-two wry poems about nasty children; and *The Forgetful Wishing Well*, containing seventy poems divided into seven sections, featuring ear-catching sounds and fresh word combinations in such poems as the title poem and "Blow-up," from the section "All Around the Year."

He also co-authored *Knock at a Star* with his wife, Dorothy M. Kennedy (see pages 141–42, 159, and 161 for discussion in this volume).

Recently he went from poetry to prose to create his first work of children's fiction, *The Owlstone Crown.*

About his writing he states, "I have never been able to write what is termed free verse. I love the constant surprise one encounters in rhyming things, and the driving urge of a steady beat."

Born in Dover, New Jersey, on August 21, 1929, he

has lived for many years in Bedford, Massachusetts. The Kennedys have five children: Kathleen, David, Matthew, Daniel, and Joshua.

"Our girl and four boys, born from 1963 to 1972, are friendly but supportive critics; and while I subtly urge them to love poetry—anybody's—I have to admit that poetry is a little farther down their ladder of love objects than quarter-pounders, ice skating, electronic rock music, and *The Dukes of Hazzard.* But such is life."

The X in his name was chosen arbitrarily "to distinguish me from the better-known Kennedys!"

REFERENCES:

One Winter Night in August and Other Nonsense Jingles. Illustrated by David McPhail. Margaret K. McElderry Books/Macmillan, 1975.

An Introduction to Poetry. Little, Brown, fourth edition, 1978.

The Phantom Ice Cream Man: More Nonsense Jingles. Illustrated by David McPhail. Margaret K. McElderry Books/Macmillan, 1979.

Did Adam Name the Vinegarroon? Illustrated by Heidi Johanna Selig. Godine, 1982.

Knock at a Star: A Child's Introduction to Poetry. (Selector; with Dorothy M. Kennedy.) Illustrated by Karen Ann Weinhaus. Little, Brown, 1982; also in paperback.

The Owlstone Crown. Illustrated by Michele Chessare. Margaret K. McElderry Books/Macmillan, 1983.

The Forgetful Wishing Well. Illustrated by Monica Incisa. Margaret K. McElderry Books/Macmillan, 1985.

Brats. Illustrated by James Watts. Margaret K. McElderry Books/Macmillan, 1986.

Karla Kuskin

HUGHBERT AND THE GLUE

Hughbert had a jar of glue.
From Hugh the glue could not be parted,
At least could not be parted far,
For Hugh was glued to Hughbert's jar.
But that is where it all had started.
The glue upon the shoe of Hugh
Attached him to the floor.
The glue on Hughbert's gluey hand
Was fastened to the door,
While two of Hughbert's relatives
Were glued against each other.
His mother, I believe, was one.
The other was his brother.
The dog and cat stood quite nearby.
They could not move from there.
The bird was glued securely
Into Hughbert's mother's hair.

Hughbert's father hurried home
And loudly said to Hugh:
"From now on I would rather
That you did not play with glue."

—from DOGS & DRAGONS, TREES & DREAMS

Whenever I think of Karla Kuskin's poetry, I think of a teacher I met while conducting a week-long workshop on poetry at the University of Nevada in Las Vegas. It was there the teacher "found" Karla Kuskin and delighted in sharing her humorous poems with the class. Each day she would come into class smiling, with one of the poet's books in her hands. "Do you know 'Hughbert'?" she'd ask. Without waiting for an answer, she would read aloud a poem, then another and another.

Karla Kuskin, a native New Yorker, was born on July 19, 1932, in Manhattan. Her love of verse stemmed from her early childhood years.

"As far back as I can remember," she told me, "poetry has had a special place in my life. As a young, only child, I would make up rhymes, which my mother wrote down and read back to me. And my father wrote verse to and *for* me. As I began to learn to read I was encouraged by my parents to read aloud. I was also fortunate that in elementary school, I had teachers who read poetry aloud and who greatly influenced my love of verse. I guess I grew up with a metronomic beat inside my head, which fortunately never left."

On writing for children she states, "One of the reasons I write for children is to entice some of them into sharing my lifelong enjoyment of reading and writing as my parents and teachers did when they communicated their own love of words to me. Instead of building a fence of formality around poetry, I want to emphasize its accessibility, the sound, rhythm, humor, the inherent simplicity. Poetry can be as natural and effective a form of self-expression as singing and shouting."

Her first book, *Roar and More*, published in 1956, began as a project for a graphic arts course she took at Yale University, from which she graduated. Many volumes of verse followed.

The poet's collection *Dogs & Dragons, Trees & Dreams* contains many of her best-loved works, which were written between 1958 and 1975 and illustrated with her lively black-and-white drawings. Through introductions and notes about her poems, she leads readers on an enchanting tour of the world of poetry, telling how and why some of the poems "happened," and how rhythm, rhyme, and word sounds combine to "stick in the mind and stay on the tongue for a lifetime."

One of these notes states:

> If there were a recipe for a poem, these would be the ingredients: word sounds, rhythm, description, feeling, memory, rhyme and imagination. They can be put together a thousand different ways, a thousand, thousand . . . more. If you and I were to go at the same time to the same party for the same person, our descriptions would be different. As different as we are from each other. It is those differences that make our poems interesting.

Some of the delights in this volume include "Lewis Had a Trumpet," about a boy who is too fond of the instrument, and "Catherine," a girl who bakes a most delicious mud, sticks, and stones cake. "I Woke Up This Morning," perfect for reading, or even yelling aloud, is three pages long, telling of a young child who wakes up and can do nothing right all day; as the child's frustrations mount, so does the type on the pages, becoming larger and larger, making the poem funnier and funnier.

Of course, there is a serious side to Mrs. Kuskin's work. Many of her poems are tender, thought provoking, reflecting various ages and stages of a child's growing up.

Mrs. Kuskin has written several highly acclaimed picture books, including *A Space Story*, which weaves together a poetic science fiction tale and a factual introduction to the nighttime sky; *The Philharmonic Gets Dressed* delightfully tells how 105 members of an orchestra prepare for an eight-thirty performance.

In 1985, she created the first original collection of verses for Harper & Row's I Can Read Book series, *Something Sleeping in the Hall*, featuring twenty-eight rhymes about various animals.

The poet lives in Brooklyn, New York. She has two grown children, Nicholas and Julia. She designed the official medallion for the NCTE Award for Excellence in Poetry for Children, and received one herself in 1979.

She has stated, "The French critic Joseph Joubert once said, 'You will find poetry nowhere unless you bring some of it with you.' To which might be added that if you do bring some of it with you, you will find it everywhere."

She can be heard reading twenty-four of her poems on

the recording *Poetry Parade* (Weston Woods). Two filmstrip sets featuring the poet are *First Choice: Poets and Poetry* (Pied Piper Productions) and *Poetry Explained by Karla Kuskin* (Weston Woods).

On *Poetry Explained . . .* she describes the principal qualities that distinguish poetry from prose and also responds to the most frequent question, "Where do you get your ideas?" The selections she reads and comments on are from *Dogs & Dragons, Trees & Dreams.*

On *First Choice . . .* her life and work are presented. Part 2 of the filmstrip features a workshop lesson giving children the opportunity to be anything they might like to be—a chair or a strawberry, a curious mouse or a baseball with a headache—and to create rhymed or unrhymed verse about such topics. A teacher's guide, photograph, brief biographic information, and ten poems reprinted from her various books are also a part of the package.

REFERENCES

Roar and More. Harper & Row, 1956; also in paperback.

A Space Story. Illustrated by Marc Simont. Harper & Row, 1978.

Dogs & Dragons, Trees & Dreams. Harper & Row, 1980.

The Philharmonic Gets Dressed. Illustrated by Marc Simont. Harper & Row, 1982.

Something Sleeping in the Hall. An I Can Read Book. Harper & Row, 1985.

Myra Cohn Livingston

WHISPERS

Whispers
    tickle through your ear
    telling things you like to hear.

Whispers
    are as soft as skin
    letting little words curl in.

Whispers
    come so they can blow
    secrets others never know.

—from A SONG I SANG TO YOU

Myra Cohn Livingston, the fourth recipient of the NCTE Award for Excellence in Poetry for Children (1980), is another poet who truly understands childhood experiences. A collection of her books rivals a good course in child development and/or child psychology. Her poems reflect the many moments and moods of growing up; they are filled with laughter, gaiety, curiosity, tenderness, sadness, and exuberance. Whether she is telling of whispers, or the fear of an earthquake in *The Way Things Are*, her use of words, her rhythms, and her various poetic forms evoke sharp moods and vivid mind pictures.

Mrs. Livingston began writing poetry while a freshman at Sarah Lawrence College in New York. She told me, "I turned in some poems, 'Whispers' and 'Sliding' among them, that my professor felt were for children. She urged me to submit them to *Story Parade* magazine; some were accepted. In 1946, 'Whispers' became my first published poem. I submitted a complete manuscript, *Whispers and Other Poems*, to several publishing houses; it was rejected. Margaret K. McElderry [then editor at Harcourt] urged me, however, to continue writing. Twelve years later I sent the manuscript back to her at Harcourt; it was accepted and published in 1958."

Since that time, the poet has created an enormous body of work.

Commenting on her work habits, Mrs. Livingston said,

"My work habits are erratic. Poetry comes in strange ways and never at the moment when one might think it should come. There are poems I have tried to write for twenty years that have never come out right. Others seem to come in a flash. Searching for the right form to express certain ideas takes time. I try to put poems away, once written, and take them out much later. Writing is not easy; it is very difficult work. Nothing that comes easily is worth as much as that which is worked at, which develops through the important process of growing, discarding, and keeping only the best.

"I had one class in creative writing in high school. I studied with Horace Gregory and Robert Fitzgerald, two great poets, while I was in college, and learned my craft well. I have since learned more, but in college I learned to discipline myself to write in forms. One cannot break rules without knowing what they are! I try to impart this same necessity for craft as Poet in Residence of the Beverly Hills School District and to those I teach at UCLA."

She and her husband, Richard R. Livingston, have three grown children, Josh, Jonas, and Jennie, all of whom are involved in the arts. Music is an important part of the family's life.

"One of our closest friends is our neighbor Jascha Heifetz [to whom her book *The Malibu and Other Poems* is dedicated]. This enables us to hear chamber music in the house as it should be heard and to be with many fine, outstanding musicians."

The Livingstons live in a villa built on three levels in the Santa Monica Mountains in California. Their view looks out across Beverly Hills down to the Pacific Ocean. "And on a clear day we can see Catalina!" Mrs. Livingston exclaims.

Her favorite possessions are her books. "I collect Joyce, Yeats, and Caldecott children's books as well as pictures, stories, and items that my children have done for me over the years. I also prize the pictures and prints illustrator friends have given me."

Mrs. Livingston was born on August 17, 1926, in Omaha, Nebraska, and moved to California when she was eleven years old. There she began her creative career as a musician and writer. She studied the French horn from ages twelve through twenty, becoming so accomplished that she was invited to join the Los Angeles Philharmonic Orchestra at the age of sixteen.

"I had an ideal, happy childhood. I had wise and wonderful parents who taught me that a busy creative life brings much happiness. Today, I am a woman with a very full life. I have family, friends, a home I enjoy, a career that enables me to stay home most of the time, the opportunity to live in an exciting community, teach writing, share poetry with children, share my ideas with teachers and librarians, collect books, do bookbinding, and pick flowers—and to keep the joys ahead of the troubles!"

Her first book with Margaret K. McElderry at Atheneum, *The Malibu*, appeared in 1972, followed by *The Way Things Are*, *4-Way Stop*, *A Lollygag of Limericks*, *O Sliver of Liver*, *No Way of Knowing*, *Monkey Puzzle*, *Worlds I Know*, and *Higgledy-Piggledy*.

In addition to writing poetry, she is a highly acclaimed,

indefatigable anthologist. Among her collections are *One Little Room, an Everywhere*; *O Frabjous Day!*; *Callooh! Callay!*; *Poems of Christmas*; *Christmas Poems*; *Easter Poems*; *Thanksgiving Poems*; *Poems for Jewish Holidays*.

In 1982, she teamed up with painter Leonard Everett Fisher to produce such unique works as *Celebrations*, *Sky Songs*, *Sea Songs*, *Earth Songs*, and *A Circle of Seasons*.

Her homage to the great nineteenth-century English humorist Edward Lear appears in *How Pleasant to Know Mr. Lear!*

I have not only read the poetry of Mrs. Livingston but have had the privilege of hearing her read poetry and discuss creative writing on many occasions. When she speaks, she has something important to say. Her poetry and thoughts about poetry are refreshing, contemporary, sometimes controversial. The poet's views and philosophy are expressed in other parts of this volume as well as in her professional volume *The Child as Poet.*

Nineteen eighty-four marked the publication of *A Song I Sang to You*, a rich gathering of over sixty poems culled from her earlier works between 1958 and 1969, with an introduction by David McCord.

A great deal more about her life and work appears in an entertaining, sixteen-page autobiography that appears in *Something About the Author: Autobiography Series, Volume 1* (Gale Research, 1986), edited by Adele Sarkissian.

Nonprint media presentations include *First Choice: Poets and Poetry*, in which she discusses her life and work, making viewers aware of their own varied feelings and how they can be used as a starting point for writing. In part 2 of the filmstrip, a workshop lesson helps young writers to use the couplet form to create a poem based on feelings, such as disappointment. Included are a teacher's guide, a photograph, brief biographical information, and eight poems reprinted from her various books published from 1958 through 1976. On a cassette tape, *Prelude: Selecting Poetry for Young People* (Children's Book Council), she shares thoughts and ideas with educators based on her lifelong experiences of writing poetry and working with boys and girls of all ages. *The Writing of Poetry* (Harcourt Brace Jovanovich) is a set of four boxed, full-color sound filmstrips, created by her, which includes Box A, "An Introduction to Poetry" and "The Tools of Poetry"; Box B, "Traditional Forms of Poetry" and "Open Forms of Poetry"; Box C, "The Voices of Poetry" and "Forms of Poetry: The Limerick." The package, which includes teacher's guides, would be useful to both upper elementary and junior high school students.

REFERENCES

Whispers and Other Poems. Illustrated by Jacqueline Chwast. Harcourt Brace Jovanovich, 1958.

The Malibu and Other Poems. Illustrated by James J. Spanfeller. Margaret K. McElderry Books/Macmillan, 1972.

The Way Things Are and Other Poems. Illustrated by Jenni Oliver. Margaret K. McElderry Books/Macmillan, 1974.

One Little Room, an Everywhere: Poems of Love (selector). Margaret K. McElderry Books/Macmillan, 1975.

4-Way Stop and Other Poems. Illustrated by James J. Spanfeller. Margaret K. McElderry Books/Macmillan, 1976.

O Frabjous Day! Poetry for Holidays and Special Occasions (selector). Margaret K. McElderry Books/Macmillan, 1977.

Callooh! Callay!: Holiday Poems for Young Readers (selector). Illustrated by Janet Stevens. Margaret K. McElderry Books/Macmillan, 1978.

A Lollygag of Limericks. Illustrated by Joseph Low. Margaret K. McElderry Books/Macmillan, 1978.

O Sliver of Liver and Other Poems. Illustrated by Iris Van Rynbach. Margaret K. McElderry Books/Macmillan, 1979.

No Way of Knowing: Dallas Poems. Margaret K. McElderry Books/Macmillan, 1980.

Poems of Christmas (selector). Margaret K. McElderry Books/Macmillan, 1980.

A Circle of Seasons. Illustrated by Leonard Everett Fisher. Holiday House, 1982.

How Pleasant to Know Mr. Lear! Edward Lear's Selected Works with an Introduction and Notes. Holiday House, 1982.

Why Am I Grown So Cold? Poems of the Unknowable (selector). Margaret K. McElderry Books/Macmillan, 1982.

Christmas Poems (selector). Illustrated by Trina Schart Hyman. Holiday House, 1984.

Monkey Puzzle and Other Poems. Illustrated by Antonio

Frasconi. Margaret K. McElderry Books/Macmillan, 1984.

Sky Songs. Illustrated by Leonard Everett Fisher. Holiday House, 1984.

A Song I Sang to You. Illustrated by Margot Tomes. Harcourt Brace Jovanovich, 1984.

Celebrations. Illustrated by Leonard Everett Fisher. Holiday House, 1985.

The Child as Poet: Myth or Reality? The Horn Book, Inc., 1985.

Easter Poems (selector). Illustrated by John Wallner. Holiday House, 1985.

Thanksgiving Poems (selector). Illustrated by Stephen Gammell. Holiday House, 1985.

Sea Songs. Illustrated by Leonard Everett Fisher. Holiday House, 1986.

Worlds I Know. Illustrated by Tim Arnold. Margaret K. McElderry Books, 1986.

Poems for Jewish Holidays (selector). Illustrated by Lloyd Bloom. Holiday House, 1986.

Higgledy-Piggledy. Illustrated by Peter Sis. Margaret K. McElderry Books, 1986.

Earth Songs. Illustrated by Leonard Everett Fisher. Holiday House, 1986.

David McCord

THIS IS MY ROCK

This is my rock,
And here I run
To steal the secret of the sun;

This is my rock,
And here come I
Before the night has swept the sky;

This is my rock,
This is the place
I meet the evening face to face.

—from ONE AT A TIME

David McCord's poetic subjects range from nature and the country to a trip to the Laundromat. He writes for both children and adults; in an interview, he commented to me on this duality.

"Poetry for children is simpler than poetry for adults. The overtones are fewer, but it should have overtones. Basically, of course, it isn't different. Children's verse sometimes turns out, or is turned out, to be not much more than doggerel—lame lines, limp rhymes, poor ideas. By and large, verse written for children is rhymed; it is nearly always brief, though an occasional poem in the hands of a skilled performer like Ogden Nash, who was a dear friend of mine, may tell a story. But poetry, like rain, should fall with elemental music, and poetry for children should catch the eye as well as the ear and the mind. It should delight, it really *has* to delight. Furthermore, poetry for children should keep reminding them, without any feeling on their part that they are being reminded, that the English language is a most marvelous and availing instrument."

Mr. McCord's first book of poetry for children, *Far and Few: Rhymes of Never Was and Always Is*, appeared in 1952, twenty-five years after his first book of poems for adults was published.

In 1977, the year he became the first recipient of the NCTE Award for Excellence in Poetry for Children, *One at a Time: His Collected Poems for the Young*, was published, a 494-page volume of verse containing works from seven earlier titles. The volume features an introduction by the poet and a very useful subject index. Beloved works such as "Every Time I Climb a Tree," "The Star in the Pail," "This Is My Rock," and "Away and Ago" are contained in this treasury.

Recent offerings include *Speak Up: More Rhymes of the Never Was and Always Is*, a volume of forty poems; *All Small*, featuring twenty-five previously published "small" poems; and a reissue of *The Star in the Pail*, twenty-six poems on subjects ranging from the seashore to the woods to the dentist's office.

Mr. McCord was born on November 15, 1897, near New York's Greenwich Village. He grew up on Long Island, in Princeton, New Jersey, and in Oregon; he was an only child.

"Long Island was all fields and woods when I was a boy," he told me. "We lived next door to a poultry farm and not far from the ocean. My love of nature began there. When I was twelve I went with my father and mother to live on a ranch in the south of Oregon on the wild Rogue River. This was frontier country then; no electric lights, oil, or coal heat. We pumped all our water out of a deep well and pumped it by hand. I didn't go to school for three years, but I learned the life of the wilderness, something about birds, animals, and wildflowers, trees and geology, and self-reliance. I learned to weather seasons of drought and weeks of steady rain. I sometimes panned gold for pocket money—a very pleasing and exciting art once you can control it! I learned to recognize a few of the constellations and to revere the nighttime sky—Orion is still my favorite skymark! I saw and experienced the terror of a forest fire. I can honestly say that I was a pretty good shot with a rifle, but I have never aimed at a living thing since I was fifteen. My love for all life is far too deep for that."

As a child, Mr. McCord was stricken with malaria. Recurring bouts of fever kept him out of school a great deal. This, however, did not stop him from graduating with high honors from Lincoln High School in Portland, Oregon, and from Harvard College in 1921. Harvard, thereafter, became an integral part of his life. Prior to his retirement in 1963, Mr. McCord spent well over forty years at the university, serving in many capacities, but principally as alumni editor and fund raiser. In 1956, Harvard conferred on him the first honorary degree of Doctor of Humane Letters it ever granted. Then-Senator John F. Kennedy received his LL.D. at that same commencement.

The poet told me how he entered the field of children's poetry.

"Two years after I finished my master's degree in English at Harvard—I had previously studied to become a physicist—I wrote a number of poems for children. One was published in the then *Saturday Review of Literature* and got into some anthologies. I seemed to know instinctively that to write for the young I had to write for myself. I write out of myself, about things I did as a boy, about things that are fairly timeless as subjects. I do not believe that one can teach the art of writing. You are born with the urge for it or you are not. Only the hardest self-discipline and considerable mastery of self-criticism will get you anywhere.

"Children still love words, rhythm, rhyme, music, games. They climb trees, skate, swim, swing, fish, explore, act, ride, run, and love snow and getting wet all over; they make things and are curious about science. They love humor and nonsense and imaginary conversation with imaginary things. I pray that I am never guilty of talking down to boys and girls. I try to remember that they are closer to the sixth sense than we who are older.

"Sometimes poems come to me full-blown—nonsense verses in particular. More often I work at them, rewriting for choice of words and smoothness. I never use an unusual word unless I can place it as a key word so that it will make the reader look it up. Poems should open new horizons. They are vistas—familiar as well as strange.

"One of my best high-school teachers once told us, 'Never let a day go by without looking on three beautiful things.' I have tried to live up to that and have found it isn't difficult. The sky in all weathers is, for me, the first of these three things."

He paints watercolor landscapes and has had several individual shows. He was once an avid amateur wireless operator and holds a 1915 first-grade amateur wireless operator's license. Mr. McCord remembers when he heard on a pocket set he had made "one of the original experiments in what we call radio broadcasting—a man playing the banjo!"

Colleagues and critics have showered praise upon his work. Myra Cohn Livingston stated, "[He] has produced a body of work which ranks highest among all poetry for children in this country." Howard Nemerov commented, "It's a rare and wonderful poet who can delight equally . . . the listening child and the reading parent." Clifton Fadiman stated, "He is both an acrobat of language and an authentic explorer of the child's inner world."

In 1983, Simmons College in Boston, Massachusetts, presented him with a Doctor of Children's Literature degree. The citation for the degree reads:

> . . . as a poet who has dedicated your life to the creation of poetry which opens the ears of children to the nuances of language and to the splendors of the world which language represents, you have spoken in a unique voice. You have brought to bear upon your work your long and thorough investigation of and fascination with the natural world, the social world, the world of the intellect, and the world of the imagination. Through your writing you have contributed to excellence in literature for children; through your teaching and speaking you have supported the urgent need for such excellence to be available to children. You have helped awaken adults to the sounds of the child's world. With the soul of a naturalist and with the gift of the poet, you have said, 'the world begins in the sweep of eye,/With the wonder of all of it more or less/In the last hello and the first goodbye.' You have conveyed this understanding to adults and to children. The poet John Ciardi has said, 'One is too few of [you] and there is, alas, no second.' It is with great pride that we award you the degree of Doctor of Children's Literature.

Mr. McCord can be heard reading twenty-three of his selected works on the recording *Poetry Parade* (Weston Woods).

On the sound filmstrip *First Choice: Poets and Poetry* (Pied Piper Productions), he discusses his life and work, treating viewers to such beloved poems as "The Grasshopper" and "Every Time I Climb a Tree." A workshop lesson with the poet suggests two topics for writing a poem—a conversation between inanimate objects and writing about being a seagull or an eagle.

REFERENCES

Far and Few: Rhymes of Never Was and Always Is. Illustrated by Henry B. Kane. Little, Brown, 1952.

One at a Time: His Collected Poems for the Young. Illustrated by Henry B. Kane. Little, Brown, 1977.

Speak Up: More Rhymes of the Never Was and Always Is. Illustrated by Marc Simont. Little, Brown, 1980.

All Small. Illustrated by Madelaine Gill Linden. Little, Brown, 1986; also available in paperback.

The Star in the Pail. Illustrated by Marc Simont. Little, Brown. Reissued, 1986; also in paperback.

Eve Merriam

A LAZY THOUGHT

There go the grownups
To the office,
To the store.
Subway rush,
Traffic crush;
Hurry, scurry,
Worry, flurry.

No wonder
Grownups
Don't grow up
Any more.

It takes a lot
Of slow
To grow.

—from JAMBOREE

Eve Merriam is a poet, anthologist, playwright, and theater director who writes for all ages. Her play *The Club* received an Obie Award. Most of her poetry for adults is concerned with her major life interests—social and political satire, and the status of women in modern society. She lives in the heart of Greenwich Village's West Side on one of Manhattan's busiest streets.

"I love it here," she says. "I find the ethnic variety of New York thrilling. And everyone is somehow larger than life, so when things go wrong here, they seem worse than they would be anywhere else. People almost take pride in having to cope."

She has two grown sons, Guy and Dee Michel. Guy, an illustrator, provided the artwork for her book of verse *The Birthday Cow*, and did the dust jacket for another, *Rainbow Writing.* Dee is a student of linguistics.

Ms. Merriam, a petite woman, filled with vim and vigor, was born in Germantown, a suburb of Philadelphia, Pennsylvania, on July 19, 1916.

"I remember growing up surrounded by beautiful birch trees, dogwood trees, and rock gardens. I enjoyed watching birds and just walking through the woods. My mother always had a great feeling for nature and gardening. I probably inherited it from her," she commented.

She left Pennsylvania to come to New York City to do graduate work at Columbia University.

"I wanted to get away from home. I wanted to meet poets and be in New York, the literary mecca. I was a born poet. While in school I had my poetry published in various school publications. I began studying for my master's degree, but one day, while taking a walk across the George Washington Bridge, I decided *not* to walk back to Columbia. I quit my studies and decided to find a job. It seemed like a good idea—but what could a poet do? I remembered reading somewhere that Carl Sandburg once worked in advertising, so I would, too. I got a job as an advertising copywriter on Madison Avenue and progressed to become a fashion editor for glamour magazines."

While working full time, she continued to write poetry. "When my first poem was published in a poetry magazine, I could have been run over!" she exclaimed. "It was in a little magazine printed on butcher paper, but it was gold to me!"

In the 1960s, she created a trilogy of books—*Catch a Little Rhyme*, *It Doesn't Always Have to Rhyme*, and *There Is No Rhyme for Silver.* In 1984, *Jamboree: Rhymes for All Times* appeared, bringing together many of her verses from this earlier trilogy as well as those in *Out Loud*, in a paperback edition. Divided into five sections, *Jamboree* features sixty poems with an introduction by Nancy Larrick, a long-time friend. In 1986, *A Sky Full of Poems*, a second paperback volume, appeared, with seventy-six selections culled from earlier volumes.

About poetry, she states, "I find it difficult to sit still when I hear poetry or read it out loud. I feel a stinging all over, particularly in the tips of my fingers and in my toes, and it just seems to go right from my mouth all the way through my body. It's like a shot of adrenaline or oxygen when I hear rhymes and word play. Word play is really central for me. I try to give young people a sense of the sport and the playfulness of language, because I think it's like a game. There is a physical element in reading poetry out loud; it's like jumping rope or throwing a ball. If we can get teachers to read poetry, lots of it, out loud to children, we'll develop a generation of poetry readers; we may even have some poetry writers, but the main thing, we'll have language appreciators.

"Writing poetry is trying to get a fresh look at something—all poetry is. It's a matter of seeking out sense memories and trying to recapture the freshness of the first time you've experienced things. A poem is very much like you, and that is quite natural, since there is a rhythm in your own body—in your pulse, in your heart beat, in the way you breathe, laugh, or cry, in the very way you speak. What can a poem do? Just about everything."

Recent volumes of her poetry are *A Word or Two with You* and *Blackberry Ink.*

Upon receiving the 1981 NCTE Award for Excellence in Poetry for Children, she offered this advice to aspiring poets of all ages.

"Read a lot. Sit down with anthologies and decide which pleases you. Copy out your favorites in your own handwriting. Buy a notebook and jot down images and descriptions. Be specific; use all the senses. Use your whole body as you write. It might even help sometime to stand up and move with your words. Don't be afraid of copying a form or convention, especially in the beginning. And, to give yourself scope and flexibility, remember: It doesn't *always* have to rhyme."

Eve Merriam can be heard on the recording *Catch a Little Rhyme: Poems for Activity Time* (Caedmon), performing a selection of poems that invite children to respond both verbally and with their whole bodies. Twenty poems are recited from various titles, including *Catch a Little Rhyme* and *There Is No Rhyme for Silver.* Among the delights are "What in the World?" "Alligator on the Escalator," "Mean Song," and "A Yell for Yellow," all of which are included in *Jamboree.*

On the sound filmstrip *First Choice: Poet and Poetry* (Pied Piper Productions), she shows students how to have fun with words. Part 2 of the filmstrip offers a dual workshop lesson—one, an introduction to nonsense words, identifying and using them in a poem; two, an introduction of comparisons via the use of similes. Included are a teacher's guide, a photograph, brief biographical information, and ten poems selected from various books.

On the cassette *Prelude: Sharing Poetry with Children* (Children's Book Council), she offers ways to both share and read poetry aloud.

REFERENCES

There Is No Rhyme for Silver. Illustrated by Joseph Schindelman. Atheneum, 1962.

It Doesn't Always Have to Rhyme. Illustrated by Malcolm Spooner. Atheneum, 1964.

Catch a Little Rhyme. Illustrated by Imero Gobbato. Atheneum, 1966.

Out Loud. Illustrated by Harriet Sherman. Atheneum, 1973.

Rainbow Writing. Illustrated by John Nez. Atheneum, 1976.

The Birthday Cow. Illustrated by Guy Michel. Alfred A. Knopf, 1978.

A Word or Two with You: New Rhymes for Young Readers. Illustrated by John Nez. Atheneum, 1981.

Jamboree: Rhymes for All Times. Illustrated by Walter Gaffney-Kessell. Dell paperback, 1984.

Blackberry Ink. Illustrated by Hans Wilhelm. William Morrow, 1985.

A Sky Full of Poems. Illustrated by Walter Gaffney-Kessell. Dell paperback, 1986.

Lilian Moore

FOGHORNS

The foghorns moaned
in the bay last night
so sad
so deep
I thought I heard the city
crying in its sleep.

—from SOMETHING NEW BEGINS

In 1967, Atheneum published Lilian Moore's first book of poems, *I Feel the Same Way*; two years later *I Thought I Heard the City* appeared.

She commented to me, "I think I wrote most of the poems in *I Feel the Same Way* on my way to work each morning. I think of them as my subway songs. Often when I seemed to be staring vacantly at subway ads, I was working intensely on a new idea. And sometimes when it didn't come off, I put it to bed at night, with a profound faith in my unconscious where the special truth I'm seeking usually begins."

Ms. Moore was born in New York on March 17th, St. Patrick's Day.

"Did you know that they have a parade on that day?" she jests. "I feel very modest about it! It's been a birthdate I have always enjoyed because this green holiday trumpets the coming of all greenery of spring and summer. Spring, since childhood, has always been a season of hope to me."

She attended public schools in New York, went to Hunter College, and did graduate work at Columbia University.

"I studied Elizabethan literature," she stated. "I wanted to teach Christopher Marlowe to college freshmen!"

She began teaching in New York City and, due to her skill in working with children who could not read, became a staff member of the Bureau of Educational Research. Here, she worked in reading clinics, wrote professional materials, trained teachers, and did research into the reading problems of elementary school children.

"When did I become a writer? Why, I can't remember when I didn't in some way think of myself as one. One of my earliest memories is of sitting on a big metal box, outside a hardware store on the street where I lived. There was a group of children around me—the friends with whom I went roller skating and sledding—and there I was telling a series of yarns. I can still remember saying, 'To be continued tomorrow!' I wrote the plays I put on in the summers I worked as a camp counselor, and of course, I guess like everyone else, I had half a novel in my drawer that it took me years to bring myself to throw out."

It was while working with youngsters who needed special help in reading that Ms. Moore began to write for children.

"I had been identified for a long time with what are called easy-to-read materials. It's true I learned from the children the basic difference between dense and open material, but I never understood why people thought that easy-to-read material for children had to be clunky and dull. As an editor, I found out later that what I sensed was true; writers often use too many words. On their way to independence in reading, young children often need easy material, sometimes for only a very short time."

Beginning in 1957, for many years she was the editor of Arrow Book Club at Scholastic, Inc., pioneering the development of the club for readers in grades four through six.

"This was one of the most satisfying things I ever did, helping to launch the *first* quality paperback book program for elementary school children throughout the United States. It was a job that brought together my experience as a teacher, my interest in children's books, my work as a writer, and my downright pleasure in the endearing middle-grader. Imagine making it possible for these youngsters to choose and buy good books for the price of comic books! It was years before I could even simmer down. Talking to me about Arrow Book Club is like taking a cork out of a bottle. Even now I remember the endless, wonderful letters from children and teachers. They made it clear we were irrigating a drought area and raising a whole new crop of readers. Whatever I may have contributed to this program was due in part to my almost total recall of the children I had known and taught. They seemed to haunt me and were specters at my side, vigorously approving or disapproving books we chose for them."

Currently, she lives in Kerhonkson, in upstate New York, with her husband, Sam Reavin. She has one grown son, Jonathan.

"I have had the best of both worlds," she says. "I grew up in an exciting city, and now I live on this lovely farm. From time to time, Sam, ex-farmer, writes a children's book, and I, an ex-city woman born and bred, drive the tractor."

In 1982 appeared a volume of her new and selected poems, *Something New Begins*, which includes fifteen new poems as well as poems selected from six earlier collections published between 1967 and 1980. The sampling is wonderful, combining her city/country living, citing images of foghorns in the bay, reflections through store windowpanes, pigeons who never sing, country scenes of chestnuts falling, a Virginia creeper that "reaches out and/roots and/winds/around a tree," and an "Encounter" with a deer.

With Judith Thurman, she compiled *To See the World Afresh*, an anthology of poems giving insight into the earth, creatures of the earth, humans and their poetry. "Section notes" and an index are appended.

The anthology *Go with the Poem* contains some ninety poems divided into ten sections selected with middle-graders in mind. Poems about sports, animals, the city, and more appear by such twentieth-century masters as Lucille Clifton, John Updike, Ted Hughes, and May Swenson.

Lilian Moore is the sixth recipient of the NCTE Excellence in Poetry for Children Award (1985).

REFERENCES

I Feel the Same Way. Illustrated by Robert Quackenbush. Atheneum, 1969.

I Thought I Heard the City. Illustrated by Mary Jane Dunton. Atheneum, 1969.

To See the World Afresh. Co-edited with Judith Thurman. Atheneum, 1974.

Go with the Poem (selector). McGraw-Hill, 1979.

Something New Begins. Illustrated by Mary Jane Dunton. Atheneum, 1982.

Jack Prelutsky

A SNOWFLAKE FELL

A snowflake fell into my hand,
a tiny, fragile gem,
a frosty crystal flowerlet
with petals, but no stem.

I wondered at the beauty
of its intricate design,
I breathed, the snowflake vanished,
but for moments, it was mine.

—from IT'S SNOWING! IT'S SNOWING!

Jack Prelutsky, prolific writer of light verse, was born in Brooklyn, New York, on September 8, 1940, attended New York City public schools, and graduated from the High School of Music and Art in New York, where he studied voice. After a brief period at Hunter College in New York City, he left to "do his own thing."

While working in a Greenwich Village music store, he began to fill up long hours by writing verses about imaginary animals, strictly for his own amusement. One day, a friend read the poems and urged him to show them to a children's book editor at Macmillan. She encouraged him to write more, but about real animals; eventually, in 1967, *A Gopher in the Garden* was published.

"When I write animal poems, some of the characteristics of the animals are probably me or my friends. I draw on many sources. I'm sure all writers do," he said. "So my sources are autobiographical but they're also from things I read, things people tell me, things I've overheard, things I oversee."

Prior to his becoming a writer of light verse, the list of jobs he held is incredible: cab driver, busboy, photographer, furniture mover, potter, and folksinger. As a tenor, he has performed with several opera companies and choruses; as an actor, he has appeared in the musical comedy/drama *Fiddler on the Roof.* He enjoys bicycling, playing racquetball, woodworking, cooking, listening to classical music and opera. In addition to a collection of almost two thousand volumes of children's poetry, he has an extensive collection of frog bric-a-brac. He and his wife, Carolynn, live in Albuquerque, New Mexico.

Since *A Gopher in the Garden*, he has written a considerable body of work including *Circus*, *Nightmares*, and *The Headless Horseman Rides Tonight*, all illustrated by Caldecott Award winning artist Arnold Lobel.

In 1983, *Zoo Doings* appeared, verses culled from his first three books, *A Gopher in the Garden*, *Toucans Two and Other Poems*, and *The Pack Rat's Day.* He has also done several volumes of holiday verse, *It's Halloween*, *It's Christmas*, *It's Valentine's Day*, *It's Thanksgiving.*

As an anthologist, he created *Read-Aloud Rhymes for the Very Young*, a collection of over 200 poems, and *The Random House Book of Poetry for Children*, which features 572 poems, including 35 of his own verses.

Recent books include *The New Kid on the Block*, *It's Snowing! It's Snowing!*, *My Parents Think I'm Sleeping*, and *Ride a Purple Pelican.*

The poet can be heard reading his own work on two recordings: *Nightmares*, a selection of twenty-four verses from *Nightmares*; and *The Headless Horseman Rides Tonight: People, Animals and Other Monsters*, which features various poems from his published works (both Caedmon).

Available from Random House are three "Holiday Read Along" cassettes featuring his verses from *It's Christmas*, *It's Halloween*, and *It's Valentine's Day.* The cassette *It's Thanksgiving* is available from Listening Library.

REFERENCES

Gopher in the Garden and Other Animal Poems. Illustrated by Robert Leydenfrost. Macmillan, 1967.

Circus. Illustrated by Arnold Lobel. Macmillan, 1970; also in paperback.

Toucans Two and Other Poems. Illustrated by Jose Aruego. Macmillan, 1970.

The Pack Rat's Day and Other Poems. Macmillan, 1974.

Nightmares: Poems to Trouble Your Sleep. Illustrated by Arnold Lobel. Greenwillow, 1976.

It's Halloween. Illustrated by Marylin Hafner. Greenwillow, 1977; Scholastic paperback.

The Headless Horseman Rides Tonight: More Poems to Trouble Your Sleep. Illustrated by Arnold Lobel. Greenwillow, 1980.

It's Christmas. Illustrated by Marylin Hafner. Greenwillow, 1981.

It's Thanksgiving. Illustrated by Marylin Hafner. Greenwillow, 1982; Scholastic paperback.

It's Valentine's Day. Illustrated by Yossi Abolafia. Greenwillow, 1983; Scholastic paperback.

The Random House Book of Poetry for Children, (selector). Illustrated by Arnold Lobel. Random House, 1983.

Zoo Doings: Animal Poems. Illustrated by Paul O. Zelinsky. Greenwillow, 1983.

It's Snowing! It's Snowing! Illustrated by Jeanne Titherington. Greenwillow, 1984.

The New Kid on the Block. Illustrated by James Stevenson. Greenwillow, 1984.

My Parents Think I'm Sleeping. Illustrated by Yossi Abolafia. Greenwillow, 1985.

Ride a Purple Pelican. Illustrated by Garth Williams. Greenwillow, 1986.

Read-Aloud Rhymes for the Very Young (selector). Illustrated by Marc Brown. Alfred A. Knopf, 1986.

Carl Sandburg

BUBBLES

Two bubbles found they had rainbows on their curves.
They flickered out saying:
"It was worth being a bubble just to have held that
rainbow thirty seconds."

—from THE COMPLETE POEMS OF CARL SANDBURG

Carl Sandburg, the son of two poor Swedish immigrants, was born on January 6, 1878, in Galesburg, Illinois, a city about 145 miles southwest of Chicago, in Abraham Lincoln country. His father was a railroad blacksmith. Mr. Sandburg was eleven years old when he began combining schooling and jobs, leaving after the eighth grade for one job after the other. He drove a milk wagon, helped in a barber shop, waited at a lunch counter, worked as a farm hand, laborer on the railroad, secretary, newspaper reporter, political organizer, historian, lecturer, and collector and singer of folksongs. He frequently toured the United States; with guitar in hand, he sang folksongs and recited his poems.

Thirty years of his life were spent preparing a monumental six-volume biography of Abraham Lincoln; in 1940 he was awarded the Pulitzer Prize in History for the last four volumes, *Abraham Lincoln: The War Years.* In 1950, he received a second Pulitzer Prize for his *Complete Poems.*

A great deal has been written about him. In 1969, the Library of Congress in Washington, D.C., prepared an eighty-three-page pamphlet entitled *Carl Sandburg* (United States Government Printing Office), which includes an essay by Mark Van Doren and sixty-five pages listing Mr. Sandburg's material in the collection at the Library of Congress.

His first published work appeared in 1904, *Reckless Ecstasy.* Only fifty copies were printed by one of his professors, Phillip Green Wright, who owned and operated a printing press in Galesburg. Three other volumes of work were printed between 1907 and 1910. In 1914, Harriet Monroe, editor of the avant-garde *Poetry: A Magazine of Verse*, received a group of nine poems from Mr. Sandburg. They shocked her. They were unlike anything she was used to reading and/or receiving. Among the nine poems was "Chicago," included in his first book for Henry Holt, *Chicago Poems*, published in 1916. Following this volume, Mr. Sandburg's writings were published at a rapid pace: *Cornhuskers*, *Smoke and Steel*, his writings about Lincoln, his famous *Rootabaga Stories* for children, and his poetry for children, *Early Moon* and *Wind Song*, all reflecting the tempo, life, and language of the everyday people he encountered.

Mr. Sandburg once said, "I glory in this world of men and women torn with troubles yet living on to love and laugh through it all."

In 1970, *The Sandburg Treasury* appeared, which includes the complete *Rootabaga Stories*, *Abraham Lincoln Grows Up*, *Prairie Town Boy*, *Early Moon*, and *Wind Song*, with an introduction by his wife, Paula.

Early Moon begins with his must-read "Short Talk on Poetry," a beautiful essay explaining "how little anybody knows about poetry, how it is made, what it is made of, how long men have been making it, where it came from, when it began, who started it and why, and who knows all about it."

Rainbows Are Made, seventy Sandburg poems that I selected, is divided into six sections, celebrating human emotions, the magic of everyday objects, nature's face mirrored in small things, wordplay, and the haunting images of the night and the sea. Each section is preceded by one of Carl Sandburg's own definitions of poetry from *Good Morning, America*; for example, "Poetry is a phantom script telling how rainbows are made and why they go away."

Within the volume such favorite poems are included as "Arithmetic," "Paper I," "Paper II," and "Phizzog"—"this face you got"—and "Circles," a seven-line free verse that beautifully sums up the white man's ignorance of the unknown as pointed out by an Indian.

Works of Mr. Sandburg appear in nearly every major anthology of children's poetry. His words are as fresh today as they were decades ago and will continue to be years hence.

The poet died on July 22, 1967, at the age of eighty-nine. Upon his death at Connemara, North Carolina, President Lyndon Baines Johnson issued the statement:

> Carl Sandburg needs no epitaph. It is written for all time in the fields, the cities, the face and heart of the land he loved and the people he celebrated and inspired. With the world we mourn his passing. It is our pride and fortune as Americans that we will always hear Carl Sandburg's voice within ourselves. For he gave us the truest and most enduring vision of our own greatness.

Mr. Sandburg's birthplace, 331 East Third Street, in Galesburg, Illinois, stands as a monument to the poet, and in 1968 Connemara Farm, where he spent his last years, became a national historic site, administered by the National Park Service. Located five miles south of Hendersonville, North Carolina, the home and grounds are open to the public. The entire house is exactly as it was when Mr. Sandburg lived there. Each year thousands of adults and children visit these memorials.

Two recordings (both Caedmon) featuring the poet and his work include *Carl Sandburg's Poems for Children*, a reading of forty-six selections, and *Carl Sandburg Reading "Fog" and Other Poems*, recorded during 1951 and 1952; this Grammy nominee includes twenty-nine selections geared toward mature listeners.

REFERENCES

Chicago Poems. Henry Holt, 1916.

Cornhuskers. Henry Holt, 1918.

Smoke and Steel. Harcourt Brace Jovanovich, 1920.

Early Moon. Illustrated by James Daugherty. Harcourt Brace Jovanovich, 1930; also in paperback.

Abraham Lincoln: The War Years. Harcourt Brace Jovanovich, 1939.

Wind Song. Illustrated by William A. Smith. Harcourt Brace Jovanovich, 1960.

The Complete Poems of Carl Sandburg. Harcourt Brace Jovanovich, 1970.

The Sandburg Treasury: Prose and Poetry for Young People. Illustrated by Paul Bacon. Harcourt Brace Jovanovich, 1970.

Rainbows Are Made: Poems of Carl Sandburg. Selected by Lee Bennett Hopkins. Illustrated by Fritz Eichenberg. Harcourt Brace Jovanovich, 1982; also in paperback.

Shel Silverstein

THE SEARCH

I went to find the pot of gold
That's waiting where the rainbow ends.
I searched and searched and searched and searched
And searched and searched, and then—
There it was, deep in the grass,
Under an old and twisty bough.
It's mine, it's mine, it's mine at last. . . .
What do I search for now?

—from WHERE THE SIDEWALK ENDS

With any group of children—anywhere—all I have to do is mention the name Shel Silverstein, and many immediately cry out, "Read 'Sarah Cynthia Sylvia Stout Would Not Take the Garbage Out.' " Or, "Read 'Jimmy Jet and His TV Set.' " Or another or another! If today's generation of children know of light verse, they *know* of Shel Silverstein.

Author-illustrator Shelby Silverstein, born in Chicago, Illinois, in 1932, has had a diverse career. His early cartoons appeared in Pacific *Stars and Stripes* while he was a G.I. in Japan during the 1950s. Years later, he was regularly published in *Playboy* magazine, creating cartoons and offbeat verses.

In 1963, when he was thirty-one, his first book with Harper & Row, *Lafcadio, the Lion Who Shot Back*, an amusing fable, appeared. In a rare interview with Jean F. Mercier, which appeared in *Publishers Weekly* (February 24, 1975, p. 50), he discussed his writing for children.

> I never planned to write or draw for kids. It was Tomi Ungerer, a friend of mine [and a distinguished author/illustrator of children's books], who insisted . . . practically dragged me, kicking and screaming, into Ursula Nordstrom's office. And she convinced me that Tomi was right; I could do children's books.

Ursula Nordstrom, the distinguished, now-retired editor of children's books at Harper & Row, was always right! She sparked the careers of hundreds of authors and illustrators, including Ruth Krauss, Maurice Sendak, Charlotte Zolotow, and countless more.

Following *Lafcadio*, a steady outpour of Mr. Silverstein's best-selling books appeared, including *The Giving Tree* and *A Giraffe and a Half.*

In 1974, *Where the Sidewalk Ends* established the author as one of America's most popular writers of light verse. *A Light in the Attic* appeared in 1981, and sold over 575,000 copies within the first year of publication. In 1985, the volume broke publishing industry records, staying on *The New York Times* best-seller list well over three years—longer than any hardcover book in the list's fifty-year-plus history. Other awards for the book include the 1984 Children's Book Award for nonfiction from the New Jersey Library Association and, in the same year, the William Allen White Award, voted upon by more than 52,000 fourth- through eighth-graders throughout the state of Kansas—the first book of verse to win the White Award in the program's thirty-two-year-old history.

About *A Light in the Attic*, Mr. Silverstein stated, "I like to think of *Light* as not an all-time best seller but as a good book."

A very private person, he has long refused to discuss his books or even allow Harper & Row to release any biographical information about him or photographs. Of course, his picture does appear on the back dust jackets of several of his books.

He lives in as diverse a manner as he writes, dividing his time among Greenwich Village in New York City, Key West, Florida, and a houseboat near Sausalito, California.

"I believe everyone should live like that," he commented. "Don't be dependent on anyone else—man, woman, child, or dog. I want to go everywhere, look at and listen to everything. You can go crazy with some of the wonderful stuff there is in life."

In addition to his books for children and adults, he is also a composer, lyricist, folksinger, and performer. His most popular song, "A Boy Named Sue," was recorded by Johnny Cash. He is also the author of several plays, including his first, *The Lady or the Tiger*, in 1981, and *The Crate*, produced off-Broadway in 1985.

Film buffs can catch his appearance in the 1971 film starring Dustin Hoffman, *Who Is Harry Kellerman and Why Is He Saying Those Terrible Things About Me?*

Mr. Silverstein can be heard on the delightful recordings *Where the Sidewalk Ends* (CBS), which includes thirty-six verses selected from the collection, and which won the 1985 Grammy Award for the Best Recording for Children, and *A Light in the Attic* (CBS), where he performs thirty-nine pieces. Adult listeners can hear him perform thirteen of his ditties on the recording *Songs and Stories*, including such riots as "Never Bite a Married Woman on the Thigh," "The Father of a Boy Named Sue," and "Show It at the Beach," produced by Parachute Records, Inc.

"I would hope that people, no matter what age, would find something to identify with in my books," he comments. "Pick one up and experience a personal sense of discovery."

In an article, "The Light in His Attic," (*The New York*

Times Book Review, March 9, 1986), poet Myra Cohn Livingston stated: "Mr. Silverstein's genius lies in finding a new way to present moralism, beguiling his child readers with a technique that establishes him as an errant, mischievous and inventive child as well as an understanding, trusted and wise adult . . . what he says in light verse and drawings to children is of such importance, such urgency that we must be grateful that more than three million copies of his books are being read. In a world that needs a generation of imaginative thinkers, may there be millions and millions more."

Undoubtedly there will be!

REFERENCES

Lafcadio, the Lion Who Shot Back. Harper & Row, 1963.
A Giraffe and a Half. Harper & Row, 1964.
The Giving Tree. Harper & Row, 1964.
Where the Sidewalk Ends. Harper & Row, 1974.
A Light in the Attic. Harper & Row, 1981.

The preceding discussions have been limited primarily to volumes of original verse. Elementary classrooms and homes should contain many volumes of original verse, along with a number of poetry anthologies. Using anthologies is an excellent way to acquaint boys and girls with a wide variety of poets and their different writing styles, and they are convenient to have on hand for children, teachers, and parents, to dip into whenever they feel the need. One of the greatest benefits of a good anthology is that its poems can satisfy many interests and levels and are balanced with work by poets of all genres.

Good anthologists strive for this variety. As the anthologist William Cole wittily remarked to me, "Any anthology done without enthusiasm is like a TV dinner—frozen, tasteless, and quickly forgotten."

Anthologies can be grouped into two categories: One, general anthologies that contain poems on nearly any subject, sometimes arranged or grouped under specific topics; and, two, specialized anthologies that contain poems on one particular subject.

Every home and classroom should have a potpourri of poetry on its bookshelves. Collections of original verse and general and specialized anthologies should be present in number. One good anthology is not enough! With many high-quality anthologies available both in hardcover and paperback editions, children of all ages can enjoy the hundreds of poems and poets tucked inside several volumes. Librarians or booksellers can suggest the more popular anthologies for use with children. But before you choose or buy, decide for *yourself* what is best for you and the children.

ADDITIONAL REFERENCES

Baring-Gould, William S., and Baring-Gould, Cecil. *The Annotated Mother Goose.* Potter, 1982.

Seuss, Dr. *And to Think That I Saw It on Mulberry Street.* Vanguard, 1937.

PART THREE

"Butterflies Can Be in Bellies!"

Sparking Children to Write Poetry

Once children have been exposed to and enjoyed poetry over a period of time, many will compose poems of their own.

Children should and can write poetry. Children's work is meant to be shared. They can read their works to one another, print it in a class or school newspaper, include it in a play or assembly program, or give it as a priceless gift to someone special.

Often, I receive letters from parents, teachers, and librarians asking me how they can get "Charlie's" poem published. The important thing should be the creation of something from within the child—and that is enough! A child's poem is not any better because it appears in print. We must not feel that everything a child writes is publisher-bound. Poems do not have to appear in print to be heard or be enjoyed by oneself, one's peers, or by an intimate group. We should encourage children to write, play with language, use words in new and special ways, rewrite, and develop their creative potential.

Writing poetry is not easy. Children should be taught to rework their creations—rework them again and again until they "feel" right.

Sound advice regarding children and the poetic experience is offered in Myra Cohn Livingston's *The Child as Poet.*

A fine volume both children and adults will enjoy is *Knock at a Star* by X. J. Kennedy and Dorothy M.

Kennedy. Over 160 poems are included by contemporary and past masters, divided into four sections to stimulate the reading and writing of poetry. All types of verse are represented—rhyme, free verse, short-verse forms. The last chapter, "Do It Yourself (Writing Your Own Poems)," gives readers ten suggestions to start them thinking. The "Afterword to Adults" offers suggestions for involving children with poetry.

A third resource is my monthly feature, "Poetry Place," which has appeared in *Instructor* magazine since 1980, containing selected poems on specific themes, a lively illustration, and a special note encouraging students to pick up their pens and pencils to write. One article, "Give Children Poetry" (*Instructor*, March 1982, pp. 36–40), suggests various ways to increase the use and enjoyment of the feature. Some of the ideas are basic; others require a little more time and planning.

Similes and Metaphors

One way to start children writing is by employing similes and metaphors.

Using similes is a good method of introducing children to techniques for coloring their thoughts; these figures of speech compare two dissimilar objects using *like* or *as.*

Give children phrases such as "as green as ———," asking them to fill in their immediate response. When I suggest this at adult workshops, I ask the audience to give *their* response. Immediately a chorus chants, "As green as *grass*!"

Laughingly, I tell the audience that if their first-, third-, or sixth-grade youngsters said that, they would call them uncreative! Yet this is a perfect response. What is greener than a beautiful patch of grass? To a child "tired answers" are really quite fresh, since every day brings experiences, new reactions, and quite naturally the repetition of many responses we ourselves had as children. To encourage other responses, ask the children to look around the classroom for things that are green, or ask a local paint store for a chart of various colors and shades they carry for the boys and girls to use. Wanda's dress, for example, might be a different shade of green from Donna's; Donald's notebook, the chalkboard, Jennifer's lunchbox, might all contain shades of green. Thus, children begin to see the many uses of shades of green and start to develop broader perspectives.

Now that they have seen green in the classroom, ask, "What else is green?" Allow students to brainstorm until they have exhausted the possibilities. Then, try another simile using something other than color, for example, "as big as ———," "as tired as ———," or "as *anything* as."

Good results can be elicited when girls and boys get, develop, and use new ideas. Things can be poetically compared via the use of similes.

From the *like* or *as* phrases, lead the children into other comparisons. "The house was as ——— as ———," "The rain was like ———," or "The book was like ———."

Third-graders have responded:

The mouse is as small as my hand was on the day I was born.

The giant in the fairy tale is as tall as a basketball player.

The lady is as roly-poly as Santa Claus' Jell-O stomach.

This, then, is a small beginning, a way to start children thinking in terms of poetic imagery, finally setting their thoughts down in pint-sized poems.

In a short but pointed article, "Age and Grade Expectancy in Poetry: Maturity in Self-Expression" (*Today's Catholic Teacher*, September 12, 1969, pp. 18–19), Nina Willis Walter discussed the fact that a child's first attempts at writing poetry are usually very simple. Even high-school students who have not previously attempted a poem may begin to express themselves at a very elementary level of writing. She reports:

> The comparison of snow to a blanket is not new, but the following poem was a creative effort by the child who wrote it because the idea of making comparison was new to him and because he was looking at the snow and saying what it looked like to him.
>
> The snow
> Is like a big white blanket
> On the ground.
>
> —JOEY BARNES, AGE 6

Rather than dismissing Joey's composition as *uncreative*, it would be better to develop with him additional ideas and feelings about snow, using other similes, and leading him into metaphors—figures of speech in which one thing is said to be another.

Metaphors abound in poetry. Share such examples as "The River Is a Piece of Sky" from *The Reason for the Pelican* by John Ciardi; "Some Say the Sun Is a Golden Earring," by Natalie M. Belting in *Piping Down the Valleys Wild*, selected by Nancy Larrick; "The Moon's the North Wind's Cooky" by Vachel Lindsay in *The Moon's the North Wind's Cooky*, selected and illustrated by Susan Russo; or William Shakespeare's "All the world's a stage and all the men and women in it merely players," in Act II, Scene 7 of *As You Like It.*

Short Verse Forms

Teachers across the country have successfully used short verse forms to call forth novel thoughts from young minds. Popular short verse forms that can be used in elementary grades include haiku, senryu, and tanka, stemming from the ancient Japanese culture; sijo from Korea; and the cinquain that originated in twentieth-century America.

Haiku In recent years, poems in haiku form have been read and written in classrooms from coast to coast. There are many reasons for the successful use of haiku with children—the poems are short, the form is easy to remember, and, with practice, enjoyable to construct.

The form was invented in Japan centuries ago; it consists of three nonrhyming lines containing seventeen syllables, five-seven-five respectively. Naturally, since the Japanese language differs from English, this form is changed when original Japanese haiku are translated.

The basic requirement of the form is that, in some way, the haiku should relate to nature or the seasons of the year. A good haiku should indicate the season from certain key words that appear within the seventeen syllables.

Another requirement is that the haiku capture a moment or a single image in the busy world of nature. A haiku should strike an image almost as if a slide had been flashed upon a screen in a darkened room.

Children of all ages can try their hands at creating haiku, concentrating and writing about a brief moment; no child, however, should be forced initially into the five-seven-five syllable limitations. I remember receiving a letter from a fifth-grade child in Michigan who was puzzled over "Hokku Poems" by Richard Wright in *The Poetry of Black America*, edited by Arnold Adoff, because two of the verses did not meet up to the "required" seventeen syllables. The required form should be suggested to students, but not rigidly enforced. The world will not be shattered if Mr. Wright's haiku, or any child's, contains eighteen syllables or fifteen! The point is to motivate all children of varying ability to express themselves in a few words and decide which words can be used to communicate poetic ideas.

Before introducing this form, read to the class a variety of haiku that pinpoint the qualities desired.

Excellent examples of haiku appear in *In a Spring Garden,* edited by Richard Lewis, a collection of classic haiku by such master writers of the form as Issa, Bashō, and Buson. The text follows a day of spring, from the early morning admonition to a toad who "looks as if/It would belch forth/A cloud," to the glowing goodnight of a firefly. The master artist Ezra Jack Keats provides vibrant collage illustrations to complement this treasure. *In a Spring Garden* is available as a six-minute film and as a sound filmstrip-book-record combination. Both are narrated by Richard Lewis, and although both are excellent, I have personally found the filmstrip package more successful for use with children in the elementary grades. You can show one, two, or several frames, allow the children to savor the exquisite collage images created by Mr. Keats, and read them the accompanying verse yourself. The film is rather fast paced; very young children might lose the mood you are trying to convey by seeing so much all at once.

There are many volumes explaining the haiku form. The best of the lot is a compact paperbound volume, *Haiku in English* by Harold G. Henderson. This book explains everything you need to know, gives many examples of haiku by master poets, and suggests lesson plans. The volume is one that every teacher should have, ready to be pulled out at a second's notice.

To motivate one lesson in writing haiku, I did the following. I brought to a fifth-grade class a bunch of jonquils and placed them in a clear vase filled with water. Alongside the vase I placed a Mason jar containing a live bumblebee, caught by one of the students in my class—

not by me! This was done prior to the morning admission bell. Several children, upon entering the classroom, noticed the fresh flowers and the bee on my desk. Other children came in and went to their desks without bothering to look at my Tuesday morning display. Soon, however, there was more buzzing in the classroom than any swarm of healthy bees could have produced. When the entire class was settled, I asked them to look at, concentrate on, the flowers and the bumblebee for just three minutes, which can be a long, long time for thirty curious creators. I told them to look at the flowers and bee as they never looked at anything before. At the end of three minutes, I carried the jar to the window, dramatically opened it, and sent Mr. Bumblebee off to freedom. I then asked the class to think about the entire experience—the flowers, the caged-up bee, and my letting it go free. I had provided them with nature, a moment, and an image.

Frieda wrote:

> The bee is set free
> But flowers, you'll only stay
> Alive for a while.

Harriet created:

> Yellow bee, Go to
> The yellow flowers outside
> Where you both are free.

Many simple objects from nature might be used to stimulate youngsters—a twig, a rock, a cricket, or a bunch of leaves. With emphasis on ecology today, haiku is a natural tie-in. Many haiku written by great masters, centuries ago, are more relevant today than they might have been at the time they were written.

Senryu Senryu, another popular verse form, is related to haiku. Named for the Japanese poet who originated the form, senryu follows the same five-seven-five pattern of haiku and also concentrates on a single idea or image of a moment. The form differs in that the subject matter is not restricted to nature or the seasons. This form gives students the opportunity to express ideas on any subject—baseball, eating spaghetti, or camping out in the woods. Below is an example of a senryu created by a second-grade child:

> The first day of school.
> Now I know that butterflies
> Can be in bellies.

Tanka Tanka are longer in form and again typically deal with nature or a season of the year. Tanka is written in five lines totaling thirty-one syllables, five-seven-five-seven-seven respectively. The first three lines are known as the *hokku*; the last two, the *ageku.* Older students will enjoy experimenting with the tanka form after they have been introduced to, and practiced, haiku.

Sijo The sijo (she-jo) verse form is a product of the fourteenth-century Yi dynasty of Korea, a period in Korean history during which science, industry, literature, and the arts developed rapidly.

The form is similar to haiku in several ways: it is based on syllabication, is unrhymed, and usually deals with nature or the seasons. In English, the form is often written in six lines, each line containing seven or eight syllables with a total of forty-two to forty-eight syllables. Originally, sijo verse was written to be sung while the rhythm was beaten on a drum or while accompanied by a lute.

One hot summer, working with a group of students in Hartford, Connecticut, I introduced the sijo form. When I asked what the group might like to write about, two replies came simultaneously: "Somethin' cold," said one child; another replied, "Old Man Winter!" Thus, thoughts of winter were conjured up in sijo form while we all melted away. One child produced:

Winter is a God-given gift
It's a pretty good one, too!
To see the white flakes falling
And cold, cold wind a'blowin'
Life seems like the seasons,
Changing with no reasons.

A boy in the group wrote:

What a gloomy, snowy night.
Dull, moody, all the way.
The ship's crew are all in fright . . .
The choppy waves roll off the coast . . .
In the galley, pots are rattling.
Storm-stopped ships on their way.

In Harlem, a sixth-grade unit on Korea incorporated the sijo form. One boy wrote:

> I wonder what's it like to
> Be a crawling caterpillar.
> They're always so alone
> And ugly and without friends, and sad . . .
> But when the time comes
> Everyone is fooled—a butterfly is born!

Again, it must be emphasized that the strict form should not be a deterrent for some children. In the examples above, you will note that the seven- to eight-syllable count per line does vary now and then.

Cinquain I was first introduced to the cinquain form in the late 1960s while visiting Frances Weissman's fourth-grade class in East Paterson, New Jersey. I immediately became fascinated with both the form and the creations that the boys and girls in her class were producing. This led to a mass of research about the form and its fascinating creator.

Cinquain is a delicately compressed five-line, unrhymed stanza containing twenty-two syllables broken into a two-four-six-eight-two pattern. The form was originated by Adelaide Crapsey, born on September 9, 1878, in Brooklyn Heights, New York.

Miss Crapsey studied at Kemper Hall in Kenosha, Wisconsin; after graduating from Vassar College in 1901, she returned to Kemper Hall to teach. In 1905, she went to Rome to study archeology. She remained in Italy for one year, returning to teach at Miss Low's Preparatory School for Girls in Stamford, Connecticut (now the Low-Heywood School for girls in grades six through twelve). The remainder of her life she fought a losing battle against tuberculosis.

The years 1913 and 1914 were spent in a sanatorium in Saranac, New York; it was here, in a room that faced an old, sadly neglected graveyard, that she wrote and perfected cinquains. Miss Crapsey termed this plot of land "Trudeau's Garden," after Edward Livingston Trudeau, an American physician who pioneered open-air treatment for tuberculosis at Saranac. This view, plus her prolonged illness, probably inspired her to write verses, both cinquain and other poetic forms, about death. One of her longest poems, "To the Dead in My Graveyard Underneath My Window," was published in 1915, a year after her death, in a slender collection of her work simply titled *Verse.*

In his preface to the 1938 edition of *Verse*, Carl Bragdon wrote of Miss Crapsey: "I remember her as fair and fragile, in action swift, in repose still; so quick and silent in her movements that she seemed never to enter a room but to appear there, and on the stroke of some invisible clock to vanish as she had come."

In my travels around the country, I have introduced this form to many children.

Although the cinquain form has been one of the most popular creative writing assignments given to children, it is also the most abused. Several recently published textbooks, as well as journal articles, pass along misinformation about the form, turning it into an exercise in grammar, writing lists of nouns, adjectives, and participles.

Three examples of perfected cinquain, as well as five cinquain sequences, a form designed by Myra Cohn Livingston, appear in her book *O Sliver of Liver and Other Poems*; fourteen more appear in her volume *Sky Songs.*

David McCord, in *One at a Time*, offers a five-page lesson on the cinquain form for readers and writers.

Like the other verse forms discussed, the cinquain allows children spontaneously to put forth thoughts and feelings in a minimum amount of words and lines. Again, the children's writing should not necessarily have to conform to the formula; overstepping the structured boundaries often enables children to write more freely.

In all these short-verse forms, children can write, experiment, and work toward perfecting poetic imagery. And through short-verse forms a child can play on city streets, bask in the beauty of the countryside, or even go to Neverland Land, as it was called by a child from Julesburg, Colorado.

Japanese Classifications of Beauty

Before or after students have experimented with and created short-verse forms, have them try their hands at forming word-pictures using the four Japanese classifications of beauty: (1) hade (ha-day), (2) iki (e-kee), (3) jimi (je-me), (4) shibui (she-bu-e).

There is no particular form for children to follow as in the above short-verse forms. The idea is to have children evoke strong imagery through word-thoughts. Students can experiment with the arrangement of words to give their images a more poetic look.

Hade signifies something that is colorful, flashy, or bright. For example:

Signs on 42nd Street
flash—
blue, green, red, yellow,
looking like fireworks
fighting hard
to explode.

Iki should portray something smart, stylish, or chic; for example:

In the window I saw
a baby diamond lying on a piece
of old, soft, blue velvet.

Or:

The bucket seats
in my brother's new car
    were
  pillow-soft
    and
  black-beautiful.

Jimi portrays images that are traditional, old-fashioned, or *seemingly* dull and commonplace:

Knife, fork, and spoon
set down on the table
for the hundredth time
wait for
the family dinner to begin.

Or:

Birds left the ground
 and took their proper pattern
for flying south once again.

Shibui, according to the Japanese, is the highest form of beauty. Here, something dull is written about but in the context of a rich background expressing joy or contrasting brightness:

The sky was pitch black
 until the lightning bolt
took over and tore it apart.

Or:

The purple pansy wasn't noticed
Until its throat turned bright yellow.

In one fourth-grade class in New York City, a teacher used the four classifications to introduce a two-month writing lesson. Each week the children were told of one classification and were encouraged to write their thoughts. After writing, they mounted their compositions on colored construction paper, illustrated them, and placed them on a bulletin board display.

In lower grades, teachers can encourage a class or small groups of children to do group exercises either independently or via the experience chart approach. In this way, children can brainstorm ideas and work and rework thoughts until perfect images are created.

Traditional Verse Forms

Children should also be introduced to such traditional verse forms such as the couplet, tercet, quatrain, and limerick.

The Couplet The couplet is the simplest form of poetry; it consists of two lines bound together by rhyme. Couplets have been written for centuries and centuries. As early as 1683, couplets were used to teach children both the alphabet and religious morals emphasizing the sinful nature of humankind. Such rhymes appeared in *The New England Primer*:

A—In Adam's fall
We sinned all.

Z—Zaccheus he did climb a tree
His Lord to see.

Many Mother Goose rhymes appear in couplet form:

> Tommy's tears and Mary's fears
> Will make them old before their years.
>
> January brings the snow
> Makes our feet and fingers glow.

Students might try writing simple verses about holidays, pets, people, food—anything.

The Tercet The tercet, or triplet, is any stanza of three lines which rhyme together. An example by Robert Browning is:

> Boot, saddle, to horse, and away!
> Rescue my castle before the hot day
> Brightens to blue from its silvery gray.

The Quatrain The quatrain form is written in four lines and can consist of any metrical pattern or rhyme scheme. In Harlem, one fourth-grader created a poem that tells a great deal about herself, includes excellent word images, and evokes a lot of thought. The child titled her verse "My Seed":

> The seed is growing deep inside
> It cannot hide, it cannot hide.
> It shoves and pushes, it bangs and kicks
> And one day the world will know me.

Ask children to hunt for examples of quatrains written by master poets and read them to the class. A collection of these can prompt discussion about how much can be said in just four lines. Some examples are John Ciardi's "Warning," depicting the dangers of a whirlpool, in *The Man Who Sang the Sillies*, or the Mother Goose rhyme that amusingly sums up the four seasons:

> Spring is showery, flowery, bowery.
> Summer is hoppy, croppy, poppy.
> Autumn is wheezy, sneezy, freezy.
> Winter is slippy, drippy, nippy.

See also David McCord's *One at a Time* for a series of quatrains.

The Limerick Limericks immediately bring to mind the poet Edward Lear, who perfected this form to amuse the grandchildren of his friend the Earl of Derby. Lear wrote many limericks, such as:

> There was an Old Man with a beard,
> Who said, "It is just as I feared!
> Two owls and a hen,
> Two larks and a wren
> Have all built their nests in my beard!"

The form consists of five lines. Lines one, two, and five rhyme; lines three and four may or may not rhyme.

After hearing many limericks written by Lear and others, children will want to create their own. To help them, you might try this: Write one line on the chalkboard, for example, "There was a man with 33 shoes." Encourage children to make up a list of all the words they can think of that rhyme with "shoes." Then they can suggest a second line for the limerick, ending with one of their words. This line is also written on the chalkboard. Next, the children can think of a third line following the thought of the limerick but not ending with a rhyming word. Now they can make a second list of words rhyming with the last word in the third line and use this as a resource to finish line four. Line five can end with a rhyming word from the first list they prepared.

The limerick form gives children an opportunity to use interesting-sounding words, experiment with language, and have fun in clever word-ways.

Collections of limericks abound. In *They've Discovered a Head in the Box for the Bread and Other Laughable Lyrics*, collected by John E. Brewton and Lorraine A. Blackburn, you will find many of Edward Lear's limericks, along with others by such notables as John Ciardi, Eve Merriam, and Ogden Nash.

Knock at a Star, by X. J. Kennedy and Dorothy M. Kennedy, presents an introduction to the form, including examples.

In Myra Cohn Livingston's *A Lollygag of Limericks*, the poet created many limericks while being enchanted by such unusual place names as Needles-on-Storr, Stroud-and-Straw-on-the-Wold, discovered on a summer trip to England. Her fine volume *How Pleasant to Know Mr. Lear!*, a tribute to the great nineteenth-century English humorist, contains a scholarly selection of Lear's story poems, limericks, notes, and artwork, divided into eleven sections. Mrs. Livingston's introduction details

Lear's life and work. Appended is the informative "Notes on the Sources of the Poems, Further Fax, and Speculations About Old Derry Downs Derry," plus an index of titles and first lines.

Twenty-seven of Edward Lear's nonsense verses are delightfully performed on side 2 of the recording *Nonsense Verse of Carroll and Lear* (Caedmon). They are read "nonsensically" by three top star-talents, Beatrice Lillie, Cyril Ritchard, and Stanley Holloway.

Arnold Lobel's *The Book of Pigericks*, original limericks in a beautifully designed volume, can further motivate writing lessons based on other animals. Can you just envision a bulletin-board display proudly touting cat-ericks, dog-ericks, horse-ericks—animal-ericks of all kinds—along with children's artwork? *The Book of Pigericks* is also available as a "Children's Literature Read Along" book/cassette package from Random House.

Parody

Children can have a great deal of fun experimenting with parodies. Limericks and Mother Goose rhymes are popular forms to use to introduce parodies. Why not have children set some of the Mother Goose rhymes in an amusement park, as Hollywood or television personalities, or at the seashore? One fourth-grader offered:

> Little Boy Blue, come blow your horn.
> The sheep's in the meadow, the cow's in the corn.
> Where is the boy that looks after the sheep?
> He's down at the seashore buying hot dogs cheap!

A fifth-grader came up with:

> There was an old woman
> Who lived in a shoe.
> She had so many children . . .
> That she looked in the Yellow Pages
> And called a Real Estate Man.

Ellyn Roe, a teacher at Cedar Heights Junior High School in Port Orchard, Washington, reports on how she uses Elizabeth Barrett Browning's, "How Do I Love Thee?" with her students on Valentine's Day.

> I read it aloud and students offer interpretations of the more difficult lines. Next the kids copy the poem's first line and proceed to list attributes of a beloved person or object. For example:
>
> How do I love thee? Let me count the ways.
> I love the way thee runs to greet me after school.
> I love the way thy coat gleams in the afternoon sun
> As I run my fingers through its furry softness . . .

Other examples of parodies can be found in *Knock at a Star* by X. J. Kennedy and Dorothy M. Kennedy.

Unfortunately, one of the finest volumes of parodies, *Speak Roughly to Your Little Boy*, edited by Myra Cohn Livingston, is out of print. If you can track it down in a school or public library, do so! In this spirited volume, Mrs. Livingston presents a wide array of poems followed by a parody and/or burlesque. Thus you will find the cumulative nursery rhyme "The House That Jack Built," followed by G. E. Bates' "Pentagonia," a clever parody about the building of the Pentagon in Washington, D.C. The poems and parodies have been largely drawn from the work of English and American poets—Edward Lear, Edgar Allan Poe, Lewis Carroll, William Carlos Williams, David McCord, and Phyllis McGinley.

Lewis Carroll was a master of parody and burlesque. In both his classics, *Alice's Adventures in Wonderland* and *Through the Looking Glass, and What Alice Found There*, many parodies appear. For example, the theologian Dr. Isaac Watts had written a four-stanza verse, "Against Idleness and Mischief," published in 1715 in *Divine Songs Attempted in Easy Language, for the Use of Children.* The verse begins:

How doth the little busy Bee
  Improve each shining Hour,
And gather Honey all the Day
  From ev'ry op'ning Flow'r.

How skillfully she builds her Cell!
  How neat she spreads the Wax;
And labours hard to store it well
  With the sweet Food she makes.

In *Alice's Adventures in Wonderland*, Lewis Carroll turned this into:

How doth the little crocodile
  Improve his shining tail
And pour the waters of the Nile
  On every golden scale!

How cheerfully he seems to grin,
  How neatly spreads his claws,
And welcomes little fishes in
  With gently smiling jaws!

There are many parodies in Lewis Carroll's writings, including the wonderful verse beginning "You are old, Father William," in *Alice's Adventures in Wonderland*, which is a close and ingenious parody of "The Old Man's Comforts," by Robert Southey.

Don't miss sharing with children of all ages the delightful recording *Nonsense Verse of Carroll and Lear* (Caedmon), performed by Beatrice Lillie, Cyril Ritchard, and Stanley Holloway. Side one consists of ten selections, including "Father William," read by Mr. Ritchard, and the wonderful interpretation of "Jabberwocky" read by Miss Lillie.

Concrete Poetry

Concrete poetry, or shape poems, are picture poems made out of letters and words; they are strongly visual, breaking away from any and all traditional poetic forms —poetry to be seen and felt as much as to be read or heard.

In Lewis Carroll's *Alice's Adventures in Wonderland*, when the mouse is telling Alice that his is "a long and sad *tale*," and she is looking down at him agreeing that his is indeed "a long and sad *tail*," her idea of the *tale* comes out this way:

Fury said to a
mouse, That he
met in the
house,
"Let us
both go to
law: *I* will
prosecute
you. Come,
I'll take no
denial; We
must have a
trial: For
really this
morning I've
nothing
to do."
Said the
mouse to the
cur, "Such
a trial,
dear Sir,
With
no jury
or judge,
would be
wasting
our
breath."
"I'll be
judge, I'll
be jury,"
said
cunning
old Fury:
"I'll
try the
whole
cause
and
condemn
you
to
death!"

Seeing Things, written and designed by Robert Froman, with lettering by Ray Barber, contains fifty-one selections arranged on the pages in shapes appropriate to their subjects. One clever bit, entitled "Graveyard," shows ten tombstones with one lettered word on each, reading: "A nice place to visit but you wouldn't live there."

REFERENCES

Adoff, Arnold (selector). *The Poetry of Black America: Anthology of the 20th Century.* Harper & Row, 1973.

Brewton, John E., and Blackburn, Lorraine A. (selectors). *They've Discovered a Head in the Box for the Bread and Other Laughable Limericks.* Illustrated by Fernando Krahn. T. Y. Crowell, 1978.

Ciardi, John. *The Man Who Sang the Sillies.* Illustrated by Edward Gorey. J. B. Lippincott, 1961; also in paperback.

———. *The Reason for the Pelican.* Illustrated by Edward Gorey. J. B. Lippincott, 1961.

Crapsey, Adelaide. *Verse.* Alfred A. Knopf, 1915.

Froman, Robert. *Seeing Things.* T. Y. Crowell, 1974.

Henderson, Harold G. *Haiku in English.* Charles E. Tuttle Company, 1967.

Kennedy, X. J., and Kennedy, Dorothy M. (selectors). *Knock at a Star: A Child's Introduction to Poetry.* Illustrated by Karen Ann Weinhaus. Little, Brown, 1982; also in paperback.

Larrick, Nancy (selector). *Piping Down the Valleys Wild.*

Illustrated by Ellen Raskin. Dell Publishing Company, reissued 1985; also in paperback.

Lewis, Richard (selector). *In a Spring Garden.* Illustrated by Ezra Jack Keats. Dial Press, 1965; also in paperback.

Livingston, Myra Cohn. *The Child as Poet: Myth or Reality?* The Horn Book, Inc., 1984.

———. *A Lollygag of Limericks.* Illustrated by Joseph Low. Margaret K. McElderry Books/Macmillan, 1978.

———. *O Sliver of Liver and Other Poems.* Illustrated by Iris Van Rynback. Margaret K. McElderry Books/Macmillan, 1979.

———. *Sky Songs.* Illustrated by Leonard Everett Fisher. Holiday House, 1984.

——— (selector). *How Pleasant to Know Mr. Lear!* Holiday House, 1982.

———. *Speak Roughly to Your Little Boy: A Collection of Parodies and Burlesques, Together with the Original Poems, Chosen and Annotated for Young People.* Harcourt Brace Jovanovich, Inc., 1971.

Lobel, Arnold. *The Book of Pigericks: Pig Limericks.* Harper & Row, 1983.

McCord, David. *One at a Time: His Collected Poems for the Young.* Illustrated by Henry B. Kane. Little, Brown, 1974.

Russo, Susan (selector and illustrator). *The Moon's the North Wind's Cooky: Night Poems.* Lothrop, 1979.

PART FOUR

"The Water's Starting to Bleed!"

A Potpourri of Poetry Ideas

This section offers dozens of ideas for motivating and appreciating poetry at home, in classrooms, or libraries. No attempt has been made to assign age levels to these projects; they can be, and have been, used effectively or adapted to fit any age level. A variety of themes tie in with children's interests and curricula. None of the projects demand excessive time or unusual materials. Items like shoeboxes, string, and Styrofoam can often be more valuable than expensive commercial kits of materials. With a little bit of imagination, and an occasional trip to Woolworth's, you will find that children will be passing the poetry often with pride and pleasure.

Mother Goose Grows and Grows

As well as being an important part of our literary heritage, Mother Goose rhymes also serve as an excellent introduction to poetry. The powerful rhythm and highly imaginative, action-filled use of words, the wit, ideas, and compact structure of the rhymes aid children in developing a lifelong interest and appreciation of verse.

A trip to almost any library will supply countless Mother Goose collections, illustrated by master artists. Not-to-be-missed volumes are listed in the "Mother Goose Collections" on pages 243–44.

Boys and girls of all ages can have a great time with the melodies, rhythm, and language, and will find that the Mother of us all can provide innumerable opportunities for many imaginative and creative activities.

Creating a Mother Goose Village After children are familiar with a variety of Mother Goose collections, begin planning a Mother Goose village. Children can be asked which rhymes they would like to dramatize, what costumes, props, and scenery will be needed. Once the projects have been chosen, the village can be mapped out. Street signs such as "Jack Horner's Corner" or "King Cole's Court" can be made by the children and placed around the room to show the locations of the various projects.

The entrance to your classroom can become a giant shoe. Let the children help decide what measurements are needed for the shoe; sketch an outline of it, and the doorway, on a large piece of brown wrapping paper for the children to paint and cut out. After the shoe is framed around the doorway, it can be decorated with photographs of the children—the inhabitants and stars of the Mother Goose Village. A sign that says "Welcome to Mother Goose Village" can provide a final touch.

For Contrary Mary's garden, paper flowers created by the children can be attached to sticks and planted in Styrofoam-filled shoeboxes, which can be set "all in a row" and covered with green crepe-paper borders. The garden can also become a birthday garden if you have the girls and boys draw daisies with brightly colored petals on plain white paper plates. The eye of each daisy can contain a child's name and birthdate. Each can be attached to a stick or colored straw and planted.

A large, rectangular cardboard box can easily serve as Humpty Dumpty's wall. Children can draw or paint bricks on the box, and Humpty can be fashioned from a large balloon. Paint on facial features with a felt-tip pen. Use cellophane tape to add a hat and a paper necktie, and then tape Humpty to the wall to await his fate. When the moment for the great fall comes, a child can pierce the balloon with a pin. Be sure that you have an extra balloon on hand as an understudy just in case Humpty explodes before his cue!

A cockhorse for the Lady of Banbury Cross can be made from a broom. A paper-bag horse face can cover the straw. Rags, crepe paper, or colored yarns can be tied around the end of the stick to make a tail.

What rhymes take place in the country? What rhymes take place in the city? Two backdrops can be planned to provide extra space for performers. A "rural mural" can include a haystack for Little Boy Blue, a meadow, a barn for the cow, and so on. A "city mural" might include some of the shops mentioned in the rhymes.

Creative Dramatic Techniques There are many ways to dramatize Mother Goose rhymes. Some can be recited by one child or a chorus; others can be sung by the children using traditional music or their own melodies. The abilities and needs of the children and the rhymes themselves will dictate the most appropriate form.

Short, familiar rhymes such as "Jack and Jill," "Little Miss Muffet," or "Humpty Dumpty" are easy to pantomime as the audience guesses the name of the rhyme depicted.

Longer narrative rhymes such as "Old Mother Hubbard" or rhymes that can be expanded, such as "Tom, Tom, the Piper's Son," can be enacted with puppets. For "Old Mother Hubbard," one child might narrate while others recreate the action and improvise dialogue for the puppet characters.

Involve one group of children in a "countdown for a cow." The cow is leaving for the moon. Present at the countdown are the Cat and the Fiddle, the Dish and the Spoon, and other animals and objects invented by the children, who can dress up in paper-bag masks. What are the reactions of the citizens of Mother Goose Village? Will the cow make it? Live interviews can also be successful with such characters as Humpty Dumpty, and the Queen of Hearts, as well as many others.

A first-grade class in Harlem produced "Mother Goose Comes to New York," in which they created their own parodies based on the popular rhymes. A third-grade class in Virginia staged a Mother Goose festival; a sixth-grade class in New Jersey held an extraordinary Mother Goose pageant, enjoyed by the entire school in the assembly hall.

Language Arts and Critical Thinking Mother Goose rhymes are full of lost or missing things—lost sheep, lost mittens, lost mouse tails. There are also many things that could be missing—Jack Horner's plum or Miss Muffet's spider, for instance. The children can draw missing objects or write the words for them on a piece of paper. These can then be placed in a coffee can or a cardboard well made from a milk carton. Each boy or girl can fish out a slip of paper and match the object with the Mother Goose character who lost it. Other children might prefer writing lost and found ads—for example, "Lost—24 blackbirds. Last seen in the King's backyard."

Many foods are mentioned in the rhymes. A classroom Mother Goose market could advertise and sell curds and whey, hot cross buns, and pease porridge hot and cold—with reduced prices for the "nine-day-old" variety! The children can make signs listing the items and prices as well as for things out of stock, such as "Sorry—No Bones Today."

What are some jobs mentioned in the rhymes? Do any exist today? What are they called? In a job-hunting game, set at a modern "employment agency," boys and girls can apply for jobs as cobblers or piemen. Can jobs be found to match their skills?

Little Miss Mouse sat on a ———. Children can create original rhymes, perhaps creating Mother Goose–type verses about their favorite television or cartoon characters.

To enhance mathematics lessons, have students note the rhymes containing numbers, encouraging them to make up individual word problems for classmates to solve. For example: How many men went to sea in a bowl? (Three.) Add that number to the number of bags of wool the black sheep had. What is the answer? Six. With numberless rhymes, children can have great fun studying various illustrators' interpretations. For example, how many silver bells and cockle shells can they find in this picture of Contrary Mary's garden? How many in that? How many children lived in each version of the old woman's shoe?

Visual literary skills are enhanced as well when students look at various illustrators' interpretations of Mother Goose characters. Which picture of Little Miss Muffet and the spider that sat down beside her is your favorite? Why?

Culminating Activities A "pat-a-cake party" can be planned when the show is over. Children can help bake cakes and put alphabet letters on the frosting or decorate store-bought cupcakes to serve at the party.

A picture map can be assembled from drawings made by the children of the various areas of Mother Goose Village. The finished map can be placed on a dittoed program sheet and distributed to visitors as a memento of the village. Map skills can be reinforced by asking questions: How can we get from one area of the village to another? What places do we have to pass? What is the best route?

Mother Goose in Recordings and Multimedia Sets Mother Goose has been treated in a number of unique ways in media. The following materials are those that have proved to be most effective with children.

Caedmon features the recording *Mother Goose*, starring three luminaries from the entertainment world, Cyril Ritchard, Celeste Holm, and Boris Karloff, who perform sixty-nine verses and songs. Both familiar and lesser-known selections are included.

Folkways has produced *Nursery Rhymes*, a recording with Ella Jenkins, the distinguished folksinger, who performs twenty-two favorite verses.

Zaner-Bloser's "Nursery Rhyme Mats" includes a boxed set of fifteen large (17½" × 11¾"), durable, plastic-laminated pupil mats with a different rhyme on each mat, illustrated in full color by Anthony Rao; the reverse side of each mat features the Zaner-Bloser Manuscript Alphabet and cardinal numbers from 1 through 10. A teacher's mat features all of the nursery rhymes on the pupils' mats. A hardcover volume, *The Highlights Book of Nursery Rhymes,* also illustrated by Anthony Rao, completes the package.

The mats can also be ordered in sets of five; *The Highlights Book of Nursery Rhymes* can also be ordered separately.

Silo's *Mainly Mother Goose Songs and Rhymes for Merry Young Souls* is a recording featuring traditional Mother Goose rhymes as well as favorite childhood songs. More than seventy selections are accompanied by combinations of fiddle, guitar, dulcimer, even knee-slapping and whistling.

Spoken Arts has produced two recordings entitled *Treasury of Nursery Rhymes.* The selections are sung, read, and arranged by Christopher Casson, the son of Dame Sybil Thorndike and Sir Lewis Casson. Volume one contains forty-two rhymes; volume two contains over fifty selections. To enhance the songs, Mr. Casson uses an Irish harp and recorder for pleasing backgrounds.

The Mother Goose Book filmstrip series produced by Random House is based on the magnificent illustrations from *The Mother Goose Book* by Alice and Martin Provensen. Six filmstrips with recordings, activity sheets, a music sheet, poster, and a hardcover edition of the book comprise this treasury.

Weston Woods features *The Mother Goose Treasury*, a filmstrip with illustrations by Raymond Briggs in full color.

Poetry Activities for All Ages

In addition to Mother Goose, try the following activities to involve children in all kinds of poetic experiences.

Best Poem of the Month At the beginning of each month, encourage students to find poems characteristic of that month. In February, for example, children might find poems entitled "February," or discover poems about Lincoln's Birthday, Valentine's Day, George Washington's Birthday, or a poem by a black poet to commemorate Black History Month. Time can be set aside each week for children to read aloud those they have found, telling why each was chosen. The poems can be written out and tacked onto a bulletin board or hanging display.

During the last week of the month, the class can vote on the Best Poem of the Month and select several runners-up. The winners can be kept in a shoebox poetry file that can serve as a good place for children to find favorite poems to read again and again. The file can also be used year after year, providing an excellent resource for future classes.

In one Texas classroom, a teacher used this idea and correlated it with a hanging calendar—a clothesline stretched across the back of the room. When the children brought in poems relating to special events—holidays, children's birthdays, local events—they were placed upon the line and labeled with specific dates. General poems about the month, such as seasonal pieces, were also attached to the line.

Another teacher using this technique held a poetry festival at the end of each month. Each of the poems selected by the class was once again read aloud—but this time to another class. Children practiced their selections; several acted them out; others used simple props for their poetry reading; and some did projects to accompany the poems.

Often, when this idea is tried, the unexpected happens. In one class, six children had April birthdays. During that month many boys and girls brought in birthday poems. The best poem in the opinion of that classroom was Aileen Fisher's "Birthday Present" in *Out in the Dark and Daylight.*

In another classroom, during December, to the hustle and bustle of the holiday season, a first snowfall, two birthdays, and several other miscellaneous events was added the acquisition of a pet hamster—and guess what poem was selected as the best? One youngster found Marci Ridlon's delightful "Hamsters" reprinted in my anthology *Surprises*, to delight both the members of the class and the teacher.

Boo Poems to Be Scared By Halloween is one of the favorite holidays on the school calendar. Children can be "safely scared" by reading poems about ghosts, goblins, witches, wizards, and other eerie creatures and characters that make appearances during the Halloween season.

Several excellent collections of "boo" poems to share with readers are available.

Hey-How for Halloween, twenty poems that I selected, pays tribute to the spine-tingling season with works by E. E. Cummings, Carl Sandburg, Myra Cohn Livingston, John Ciardi, and others. Janet McCaffery's black-and-white illustrations capture the Halloween mood. A double-page spread within the text depicting a flock of bats flying from the moon can be used to spark children's original verse. Place the spread on an opaque projector to motivate young writers.

In the Witch's Kitchen, compiled by John E. Brewton, et al., is a gathering of forty-six poems. Ghouls, ghosts, skeletons, and spooks parade through the pages in works by X. J. Kennedy, Shel Silverstein, Theodore Roethke, Lilian Moore, and others.

Shrieks at Midnight, selected by Sara and John E. Brewton, contains poems about restless spirits roaming the earth and modern ghosts who were "done in" for daring to fold up an I.B.M. card. Poems by Lewis Carroll, John Ciardi, and Langston Hughes scare readers of all ages.

Eight delightful verses by Lilian Moore can be found in *Something New Begins.*

Thirteen easy-to-read poems appear in *It's Halloween* by Jack Prelutsky. "Skeleton Parade," "Bobbing for Apples," and "The Haunted House" are among the offerings.

Although not specifically Halloween in theme, readers will be spooked by Jack Prelutsky's *Nightmares* and *The Headless Horseman Rides Tonight.* Twelve poems appear in each volume, versifying such creatures as "The Dragon of Death," "The Bogeyman," "The Poltergeist," and "The Zombie."

Creatures, my volume, offers eighteen poems, including "The Old Wife and the Ghost" by James Reeves, "The Dracula Vine" by Ted Hughes, and "The Seven Ages of Elf-Hood" by Rachel Field.

A must for mature readers is Myra Cohn Livingston's *Why Am I Grown So Cold?* In her brief introduction, Mrs. Livingston states: "Science has many explanations for many phenomena, but it has yet to unravel many mysteries. And these mysteries are the blood and bone of this anthology." Over one hundred fifty poems give a wide array of verse dealing with the supernatural. Titles of the twelve sections are intriguing unto themselves—for example, "Enchantment, Witchery, Sorcery, Allurement, and Necromancy"; "White Wands, a Haunted Oven, The Mewlips, and Other Strange Matters." The book's title stems from "The Warning," a cinquain written by Adelaide Crapsey in the early 1900s. Indexes of titles, first lines, authors, and translators are appended.

Play a recording of some eerie music on Halloween Day with the lights turned out and a candle flickering on your desk to bring on delightful shivers.

Boxes and Poetry The sides of a small cardboard box provide ample opportunity for displaying children's interpretations of favorite poems. Secure the cover on the box with tape. Children can paint the surface or decorate the box with cloth or paper. After they have selected a poem, they can mount illustrative material on all six sides of the box. One sixth-grade student brought in a commercial photo cube, an inexpensive plastic cube available in most novelty stores. A Polaroid camera was used to shoot photographs of a New York harbor, and the finished pictures were placed in the photo cube to dramatically depict "Waterfront Streets" by Langston Hughes from *Selected Poems.*

To enrich a unit on the zoo, a second-grade teacher used shoeboxes to represent animal habitats. The insides of the shoeboxes were painted, interesting paper provided collage landscapes, and, finally, animal drawings were put into the shoeboxes. Several of the children's works were very humorous. Henry's giraffe, for example, projected through a slit in the top of the shoebox that insured room for Mr. Giraffe's very long spotted neck; Edith's elephant's trunk was far too long for the shoebox —thus it protruded through the side of the box; Roy's lion's tail stuck out through a slit in the side of the box, and a tiny paper mouse rested on the tail.

Poems about the various animals were found and placed alongside the children's artwork.

During various box-projects, be sure to share Carl Sandburg's delightful free verse "Boxes and Bags," in *Rainbows Are Made: Poems by Carl Sandburg*, in which

"Elephants need big boxes to hold a dozen handkerchiefs."

Poems about Building A New Jersey teacher correlated poetry and art for a unit on community planning and construction. The poems included Eve Merriam's "Bam, Bam, Bam," from *Jamboree*, and "Construction Job" and "A Time for Building," both from *A Song I Sang to You*, by Myra Cohn Livingston.

The teacher encouraged the children to bring back to class a variety of materials gathered at a nearby building site. Bricks, scraps of wood, nails, and plaster were used by the class to construct sculptures and collages. Finished projects were put together in a hall display.

A trip to any community site—even a junkyard—can spark children to create poetry. Sharing a free-verse poem such as "Passing by the Junkyard" by Charles J. Egita, from my collection *A Song in Stone*, can start you thinking about "heaps" of possibilities.

Choral Speaking Choral speaking is an activity that can contribute to the appreciation and enjoyment of poetry as well as provide worthwhile learning and listening experiences.

The easiest form of choral speaking is the refrain, where children merely repeat the refrain of a frequently repeated line of a longer poem. After hearing a selection several times, children quickly note that the line will appear and reappear, and they will wait anxiously for their cue to participate.

I have used, for example, Shel Silverstein's "Peanut Butter Sandwich" from *Where the Sidewalk Ends* with boys and girls in preschool and kindergarten classes. Each of the twelve stanzas ends with the words "peanut butter sandwich." Before reading the selection, I ask them to shout out the three words. I next tell them that when I raise my hand this is the cue for them all to shout "peanut butter sandwich." It has never failed me. With the availability of the recording based on the book (CBS), children can shout out the words along with Mr. Silverstein, if you don't want to read it aloud.

A second type of arrangement is two-part speaking. Two groups of children take a part of the poem. An example is the nursery rhyme:

RIDING

This is the way the ladies ride:	GIRLS
Tri, tre, tre, tree: tri, tre, tre, tree!	ALL
This is the way the ladies ride:	GIRLS
Tri, tre, tre, tree: tri, tre, tre, tree!	ALL
This is the way the gentlemen ride:	BOYS
Gallop-a-trot, gallop-a-trot!	ALL
This is the way the gentlemen ride:	BOYS
Gallop-a-trot, gallop-a-trot!	ALL
This is the way the farmers ride:	BOYS
Hobbledy-hoy, hobbledy-hoy!	GIRLS
This is the way the farmers ride:	BOYS
Hobbledy-hoy, hobbledy-hoy!	GIRLS

Line-a-child arrangements are somewhat difficult, yet give each child a chance to speak one or more lines alone. The difficulty arises from the necessity for precision of delivery.

In part-speaking, varied groups of children take parts of the selection. The teacher has the responsibility of knowing which child can handle the various speaking assignments. One example:

IF YOU'RE GOOD

Santa Claus will come tonight	BOYS
If you're good	ALL
And do what you know is right	GIRLS
As you should.	ALL
Down the chimney he will creep,	SOLO
Bringing you a wooly sheep	SOLO
And a doll that goes to sleep	SOLO
If you're good.	ALL
Santa Claus will drive his sleigh	BOYS
Through the wood	ALL
But he'll come around this way	GIRLS
If you're good.	ALL
With a wind-up bird that sings	SOLO
And a puzzle made of rings,	SOLO
Jumping jacks and funny things.	ALL
If you're good.	ALL
He will bring you cars that go	BOYS
If you're good	ALL
And a rocking horsey, oh,	GIRLS
If only he would!	SOLO

And a dolly that can sneeze,	SOLO
That says, "Mama!"	
when you squeeze	SOLO
He'll bring you some of these	SOLO
If you're good.	ALL
Santa grieves when you are bad,	BOYS
As he should:	ALL
But it makes him very glad	SOLO
When you're good;	SOLO
He is wise and he's a dear	SOLO
Just do right and never fear	SOLO
He'll remember you each year—	SOLO
If you're good!	ALL

The most difficult type of choral speech is unison speaking, for it involves all students speaking at the same time. Perfect timing, balance, phrasing, inflection, and pronunciation are required, which takes much practice and is quite time-consuming.

Programs of choral speaking can be planned and enhanced with lighting effects and with interesting staging techniques, such as having children stand in a semicircle, scattering them around the stage, or interspersing simple dance and mime with their readings.

Choral speaking helps develop good speech, provides the timid child with a degree of self-confidence, and gives many pleasurable moments.

Circus! Circus! Who can resist the magic of the circus? Color, lights, action, music, clowns, acrobats, animals, and a host of other sights and sensations constitute a circus atmosphere full of many poetic images. If your students have never seen a real three-ring entertainment, you can bring it alive in the classroom.

Jack Prelutsky's *Circus* contains poems about aerial acrobats, monkey bands, equestrians, and clowns that prance through the pages as "the circus parade goes marching."

More fun and rhymes are available in *If I Ran the Circus* by Dr. Seuss, and *You Think It's Fun to Be a Clown!* by David Adler. Don't miss Ray Cruz's full-color pictures in this volume featuring clowns that leap from the pages. The witty, surprise ending is a special treat.

Add musical zest to circus festivities by using selected songs from the Broadway musical *Barnum*, available at your local record shop on a CBS recording.

For additional ideas on using the circus theme, write for *Circus—A Teaching Unit*, a twenty-four-page booklet that provides background information and a variety of teaching suggestions that cover all curriculum areas. Single copies are available free from Ringling Brothers and Barnum and Bailey Circus, Department of Educational Services, 3201 New Mexico Avenue, N.W., Washington, D.C. 20016.

Blow up some balloons, pop some popcorn, put out some clown makeup, play *Barnum*, and display the books of circus poems to let the world know that the circus is coming to your classroom.

Collage Poetry Balls After children have selected a favorite poem, encourage them to create a collage poetry ball. Children's collages interpreting the poem can be placed on large circles cut from oaktag or construction paper. Photographs from newspapers or magazines, cloth, realia, various sizes of print or type, and original drawings can be the raw material for depicting the poem's meaning.

Shirley McCammon, an English teacher, used a variation of this idea to encourage her students to write poetry. "I Am" collages motivated students to ask themselves, "Who am I? Where am I going? Where did I come from?" After the collages were completed, students wrote several sentences about themselves, leading to the creation of free verse after they had worked and reworked their original lists. One example follows.

List of Sentences:

> I am inhibited to degrees.
> Filled with mixed emotions.
> Unhappy at times, full of life.
> Lonely but popular.
> I am one and the same.
> I am unique.
> I am ME!

The verse:

> Inhibited, filled with emotions,
> Unhappy at times,
> Though full of life.
> Lonely, yet popular,
> I am uniquely ME.

Children can create collages focusing on their homes, families, special interests, hobbies, pets, peers, or aspirations; they can then try writing poems about themselves and their collage constructions.

These can also be turned into poetry wall hangings. Children can mount wallpaper on large, rectangular pieces of cardboard and then illustrate their interpretation of poems with collage materials. The panels can be used for hall or classroom bulletin board displays, and later taken home by students to share with families.

Color Me Poetry There are a number of successful ways to involve children with finding or writing poems about color. One teacher placed a bright array of colored wrapping tissue on a bulletin board display with the caption "Find a Poem About Me."

A dramatic technique for stimulating children to think about color is to use an overhead projector. Place a clear bowl of water atop the projector—a plastic turtle dish or a clear glass pie plate works best. By dropping a few drops of food coloring in the bowl, magical things happen on the screen. The coloring can be stirred around or blown to create movement, or colors can be mixed together to make new color combinations.

In a kindergarten class where this was done, one small lad remarked, "Oh, my! The water's starting to bleed!"

The movement of the color can be enhanced by the playing of a musical selection or can be combined with dance and rhythm movements.

Paint blots is another technique that works well. Children can drop a few blobs of tempera paint on construction paper and carefully fold the paper in half. When it is opened, they will find an interesting paint blob, à la Rorschach. Within the next few days they can give a title to their creation and look for appropriate poems that best illustrate their blots. The results will be surprising.

In *Hailstones and Halibut Bones* by Mary O'Neill, twelve poems about various colors appear, each asking a question: "What Is Gold?" "What Is Red?" "What Is Orange?" The poems not only tell about the color of objects but touch upon the ways color can make us feel, for example: "Orange is brave/Orange is bold"; "Gold is feeling/Like a king"; "Blue is feeling/Sad or low."

The poems stir our senses and make us want to look around carefully to see everyday colors we have taken for granted and see them anew in fresh, poetic imagery. To further encourage children to create color images, bring to class specific objects—a rose, a bunch of colored leaves, or a black ant; their physical presence will awaken mental images.

A Las Vegas, Nevada, teacher asks her students to describe thoughts about colors, not often written about. She asks, "How do certain colors make you feel?" Several responses include:

Aqua makes me feel like a mermaid dancing in the sea.

Bronze makes me feel like a dead statue.

Amber makes me feel like millions of waves of grain.

Color is around and about us. Use it to broaden children's writing.

Fingers on Hand Boys and girls can try creating poems about their fingers or fingers of friends, relatives, or pets. In a New Jersey classroom, a third-grade teacher did a bulletin-board display entitled "Our Fingers." Children traced the outline of one hand on a piece of construction paper. Their poems were printed on the outline and pasted onto the display. The following example is an unsophisticated verse, but a good one considering it came from a child who had never written poetry before:

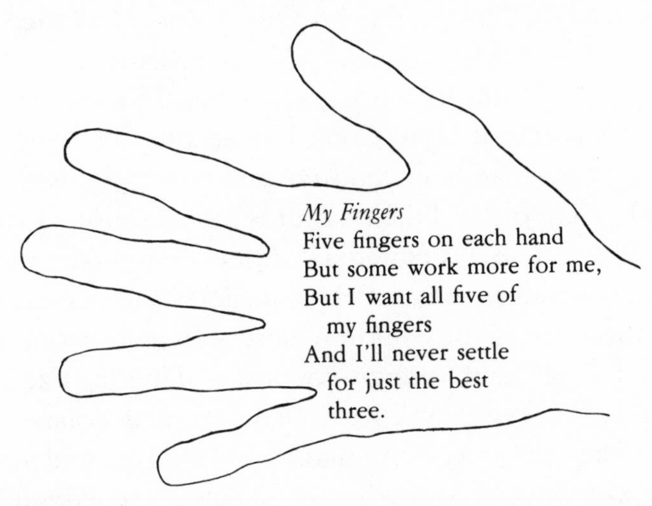

Globe-trotting with Poetry Poetry reflects people, their lifestyles, experiences, dreams, feelings, ideas. It is a universal form of creative communication, yet each poem has a unique "personality." By learning what poets from all over the world have to say, children can better understand how all people are alike and yet different.

A world-poetry hunt is a good way to start globe-trotting. Post a map of the United States and the world on a bulletin board. Underneath, set up a table display of books featuring poetry of both American and foreign poets. As the children find, read, and share the selections, they can mark off places on the maps where the verses originated.

Encourage each student to research the part of the country that his or her favorite poet comes from. Sometimes this information is readily found on book jackets. As children's repertoires grow, they will begin to see that poets come from all walks of life and environments. Some leading American poets they will want to encounter are David McCord from Massachusetts; Eve Merriam, New York; Gwendolyn Brooks, Illinois; Aileen Fisher, Colorado; Myra Cohn Livingston, California.

Poetry that can help children gain new insights about world neighbors and their cultures can be found in *Have You Seen a Comet?*, edited by Anne Pellowski, et al., which contains poems, letters, anecdotes, stories, essays, and illustrations by children and teenagers from the United States and foreign countries—Liberia, Czechoslovakia, Turkey, Costa Rica, Malaysia, and Poland.

Another attractive combination of language and verse is *Chinese Mother Goose Rhymes*, selected and edited by Robert Wyndham. Designed to read vertically, Chinese calligraphy ornaments the margins of each page. Forty traditional rhymes, riddles, lullabies, and games that have amused children for generations are included.

Perhaps groups of children would like to design and make mini-anthologies as gifts to next year's incoming class, the school library, or parents. One group might plan a poetry atlas featuring poems from continent to continent and illustrate them with original drawings and appropriate sections cut from world maps.

Growing with Poetry A primary teacher in Trenton, New Jersey, uses a chart titled "I Am Getting Bigger" in her classroom. Inches are marked off on the chart, and a space alongside the numbers records the children's names. Once a month, each child is measured to record growth. The chart contains a variety of pictures and poems to be read to or by boys and girls while their heights are being recorded. Poems might include Karla Kuskin's "The Question" in *Dogs & Dragons, Trees & Dreams*, the section "Mostly Me" in Myra Cohn Livingston's *A Song I Sang to You*, the section "Children" in Eve Merriam's *Jamboree*, or the section "At the Top of My Voice" in my collection *Surprises.*

A Line of Poetry A New York City teacher devised a good way to prompt children to search for poems by stringing a clothesline across the classroom and attaching brown manila envelopes to it with clothespins. Pictures were pasted to the face of each envelope—a picture of a boy, a girl, or an animal, or a photograph depicting a particular season of the year. Class members were encouraged to look for, or write, poems about the illustrations on the envelopes and put them into the envelopes. A poetry clothesline can become a permanent fixture in the classroom and be changed as often as needed to tie in with specific lessons.

A Peephole Poetry Display Students can let their imaginations run wild when creating peephole poetry displays, working individually or in groups. After a poem has been selected, a hole about the size of a pencil should be punched in one end of a shoebox, while the other end is cut out completely and covered with cellophane. The children then construct a diorama inside the box interpreting the poem selected. When the display is completed, the boxtop is put on and the light from a flashlight is projected through the cellophane. As one child reads the poem, or it is read on a commercial or class-made recording or tape, another can peep through the hole and view the diorama.

People Poems Poems about people of every size, shape, and form are indeed plentiful in the world of children's poetry.

Readers can encounter friends such as Sarah Cynthia Sylvia Stout, who "would not take the garbage out," or Benjamin Bunnn, "whose buttons will not come undone" in Shel Silverstein's *Where the Sidewalk Ends.*

Lewis, who "had a trumpet," Hughbert, and Alexander Soames, a child who speaks only in rhyme, are three characters in Karla Kuskin's *Dogs & Dragons, Trees & Dreams.*

For mature readers, Nancy Larrick offers a bountiful collection, *Crazy to Be Alive in Such a Strange World.*

Famous people are also the subjects of many poems. An excellent collection to have on hand is Rosemary and Stephen Vincent Benét's *A Book of Americans*, featuring such personalities as Johnny Appleseed, Dolly Madison, P. T. Barnum, and the Wright Brothers, perfect for enhancing American history lessons.

In the section "Grownups" in Eve Merriam's *Jamboree*, we meet Abraham Lincoln, George Washington, and King Solomon.

After hearing and reading a variety of people poems, students might think of people they would like to meet and write about—the school custodian, a favorite teacher, the local pet shop owner, a pizza maker—anyone, either famous or not. Finished poems might be given to favorite people as a gift.

Personal Poetry Anthologies Dianne Weissberger, a teacher in Germantown High School, Germantown, Pennsylvania, excited her students by sending them on a poetry hunt. The students selected a theme, finding ten related poems; these were transcribed into booklets, illustrated with appropriate pictures. On the last page of each booklet, the students wrote a concluding paragraph explaining why they had chosen a particular theme and how they felt about it while working on the project. Ms. Weissberger reports: "The summary paragraphs proved to me that students gained much insight into themselves and actually found poetry fun!"

The number of poems selected can depend on age level. Third-graders, for example, might choose only three or four poems relating to a specific topic.

The basic objective is to get children to think through the whys, whats, and hows of the project. Why did they choose the theme they did? What sources did they draw from? What relationships did they see between the selections? How did they benefit from the project? Choosing poems helps children focus attention on what they are reading and feeling!

Illustrations can be original drawings or pictures collected from a variety of sources. Artwork for booklets might also be created by older students, or even someone from the child's immediate family. Finished booklets might include an attractive cover containing a good title for the work and the name of the compiler and artist. A table of contents can be included as well as an index of titles, first lines, and poets, all reinforcing important language arts skills. To add to this project, students might include a brief biographical sketch of each poet. The last page can contain a photograph of the compiler along with a composition explaining the work.

Pet a Poem Set up a class pet shop. Have children bring in stuffed toys or, under supervision, a live pet. Students can find poems to honor favorite pets, or create original poems.

Poems about pets abound. Cat lovers will find a host of feline favorites in two books of original verse by Beatrice Schenk de Regniers, *This Big Cat and Other Cats I've Known* and *So Many Cats.*

Mature readers will want to read the classic cat-of-cats book, T. S. Eliot's *Old Possum's Book of Practical Cats*, or listen to the cassette produced by Caedmon with readings by Sir John Gielgud and Irene Worth.

Twenty-four selections by nineteen poets appear in my compilation *I Am the Cat*, following the feline's life from the birth of a kitten to cats in old age.

A Dog's Life also presents a life cycle from puppyhood to a dog's death; twenty-three poems, selected by me, depict a wide array of breeds. William Cole's *Good Dog Poems* contains eighty-eight verses divided into ten sections.

Horses are heralded in *My Mane Catches the Wind*, for which I selected twenty-two poems showing life cycles from the birth of a foal to an aged horse. *The Poetry of Horses*, selected by William Cole, features 111 selections, divided into nine sections.

A pet mouse will become more alive by sharing various poets' thoughts about mice. A rich gathering of fifty poems appears in Vardine Moore's *Mice Are Rather Nice.*

All four creatures are celebrated in Part 8 of Nancy Larrick's *Piping Down the Valleys Wild*, via twenty-two selections. Parrots, monkeys, turtles, and goldfish are also mentioned.

A Picture for a Poem Dig into your own personal picture file and post an interesting photograph or picture on the bulletin board. Students can hunt for poems they feel fit the mood or describe the illustration. Catchy titles add to such displays. For example, the caption "Sneak into This Haunted House," under an illustration of an old house—the "hauntier" the better—might elicit original poems, or a poem such as "The Haunted House" in *Nightmares*, by Jack Prelutsky, might be shared.

Other pictures and captions might deal with nature, the environment, space, sports, or the sea.

A Pocketful of Poems Cut out several large pocket shapes from medium-weight cardboard or oaktag. These pockets can be painted with tempera or covered with patterned fabric or construction paper. Label each pocket with a category such as "Me," "The City," "Insects," or "Animals." Leaving the tops open, secure the pockets to a bulletin board by stapling around the edges. Insert several poems in each pocket and encourage the children to pick out and read a poem whenever they have some free time. Near the bulletin board, place a copy of Beatrice Schenk de Regniers' "Keep a Poem in Your Pocket," from her book *Something Special.* The poem is reprinted on page 56.

Children can be encouraged not only to pick the pockets but to fill them once in a while, too!

A Poem for a Picture Students are often asked to illustrate poems they have read or heard. You might try turning this idea around by encouraging boys and girls to draw or paint a picture first, then find a poem that goes with it. Several children can look for poems they feel appropriate for a classmate's drawing. If they cannot find a suitable poem, they may decide to write their own. In any case, the children will have looked at a variety of poems, and the next time they paint they may remember just the right verse to accompany their pictures.

Poems to Satisfy Young Appetites A bulletin board can feature the question "What's for Lunch?" A table setting can be depicted by stapling a paper tablecloth on the bulletin board for a background along with paper plates, cups, and plastic cutlery. The latter can be mounted with double-faced masking tape or strong glue.

On each plate a food poem can appear. One might describe eating an ice cream cone on a hot summer's day, another might mention the spicy taste of chili con carne or relishes on a hot dog. Before lunch hour, either a child or the teacher can read a selection from the plate. The poems can be changed as regularly as children's tastes.

Three volumes of poems about food are *Eats: Poems*, an original book of verse by Arnold Adoff, which includes poetic morsels on Chinese food, chocolate, and apple pie; my collection *Munching: Poems About Eating*, featuring such tasty delights as "Bananas and Cream" by David McCord, "Turtle Soup" by Lewis Carroll, and "The Pizza" by Odgen Nash; for older readers, *Poem Stew*, selected by William Cole, offers a feast of funny poems from the creased prune to rhinoceros stew, with works by Kaye Starbird, Richard Armour, and six by Mr. Cole himself.

Poems to Celebrate Holidays hold a special place in all of our hearts, each rich in tradition. Both Thanksgiving, inherited from the Pilgrims, and Independence Day, commemorating the birthday of our country, provide us with a sense of being, connecting us with our early history and customs; Christmas and Easter are joyous days that are shared with people the world over; St. Valentine's Day and Halloween, though not considered legal holidays, bring to us hundreds of years of culture and custom, wit and wisdom, folklore—and fun!

Luckily, poetry about these and other major and minor holidays abounds. Here is a holiday potpourri sampling for you to share with students of all ages.

Harcourt Brace Jovanovich Holiday Poetry series includes six collections compiled by me: *Beat the Drum, Independence Day Has Come*; *Easter Buds Are Springing*; *Good Morning to You, Valentine*; *Hey-How for Halloween*; *Merrily Comes Our Harvest In: Poems for Thanksgiving*; *Sing Hey for Christmas Day.*

Myra Cohn Livingston's collections for holidays include *Callooh! Callay! Holiday Poems for Young Readers* and for middle-graders, *Christmas Poems*, *Easter Poems*, *Thanksgiving Poems*, *Poems of Christmas*, *Poems for Jewish Holidays* and *O Frabjous Day! Poetry for Holidays and Special Occasions.* All ages will enjoy her original creations, representing sixteen landmark days on the calendar, in *Celebrations*, including "Martin Luther King Day," "Saint Patrick's Day," "Passover," and "Birthday."

Jack Prelutsky's original verses appear in *It's Halloween*, *It's Christmas*, *It's Thanksgiving*, *It's Valentine's Day.*

Through such volumes, readers will meet works by "old-timers" such as Joyce Kilmer, William Shakespeare, and Stephen Vincent Benét; they'll find the contemporary voices of David McCord, Aileen Fisher, and Shel Silverstein; they'll weave in and out of old-new voices, too—poets who have been read by generation after generation of children and still speak to us today, such treasured poets as Langston Hughes, Carl Sandburg, and Dorothy Aldis.

Holiday celebrations can be enhanced when girls and boys design their own greeting cards. Appropriate poems can be selected or written, illustrated, and sent on such occasions as birthdays, Mother's Day or Father's Day—ideal times to write and illustrate greeting card verses for special friends and relatives.

Poet of the Month Being introduced to new poets and their work can be stimulating for children. Use a bulletin board and tabletop display to highlight a particular poet of the month. The bulletin board can feature biographical information along with several of the poet's poems printed on oaktag. If possible, a photograph of the poet can be included. A table display can feature volumes of the poet's work, and, if available, a recording of his or her voice or that of another person reading from the poet's works.

Each day, read a selection or two from the featured books and play the recordings. Encourage children to look for additional biographical information on the poet, or to search out more examples of his or her work. Build up a "poet's file" by having the boys and girls write letters to publishers or to living poets themselves requesting additional information. In the latter case, the children's letters should be sent in care of the publishing house along with a self-addressed stamped envelope; they will be forwarded to the poet by the editor. Students can also look for information in books and periodicals.

Below is a listing of poets and their birthdates. All of

these individuals are perfect choices for your students' poet of the month:

January
6 Carl Sandburg
13 N. M. Bodecker
18 A. A. Milne

February
1 Langston Hughes

March
2 Dr. Seuss
17 Lilian Moore
26 Robert Frost

April
22 William Jay Smith
26 William Shakespeare

May
12 Edward Lear
17 Eloise Greenfield
25 Theodore Roethke
31 Elizabeth Coatsworth

June
6 Nancy Willard
7 Gwendolyn Brooks
7 Nikki Giovanni
24 John Ciardi
26 Charlotte Zolotow
27 Lucille Clifton

July
15 Arnold Adoff
17 Karla Kuskin
19 Eve Merriam

August
16 Beatrice Schenk de Regniers
17 Myra Cohn Livingston
19 Ogden Nash
21 X. J. Kennedy

September
8 Jack Prelutsky
9 Aileen Fisher
24 Harry Behn

October
14 E. E. Cummings
29 Valerie Worth

November
13 Robert Louis Stevenson
15 David McCord

December
10 Emily Dickinson

A PoeTree Branches can be arranged to create a "Poe-Tree" by attaching them to a wall, hung from the ceiling like a mobile, or placed in a pail or flowerpot filled with sand, earth, or styrofoam. Spray paint can change the color of the branches from time to time.

As children select and illustrate favorite poems, they can be attached to the branches for others to read. The PoeTree can tie in with specific curriculum subjects or have a theme assigned to it.

A New York City teacher combines this idea with Poet of the Month (see page 199). Atop the tree the poet's name is printed on oaktag; when available, a picture of the poet is added. The branches of the tree are then filled with poems by the poet being honored.

The PoeTree can also be a seasonal tree. At Christmas-time, for example, Christmas or winter poems might appear; in February, the PoeTree can help celebrate Black History Month by featuring poems by or about famous black personalities.

In New Jersey, a fourth-grade teacher has each child create mini-PoeTrees as gifts for Mother's Day. Each child decorates a cardboard milk carton, fills it with earth, and places a small twig firmly inside. A poem or two is attached to the twig. At the top of the branch some children place pictures of their mothers or themselves. The mini-PoeTrees are unique, unusual, inexpensive, and very effective presents.

A Poetry Animal Fair Use a corner of the room to set up a poetry animal fair. Hang a mobile from the ceiling featuring pictures of animals. Place a large wooden box under the mobile to hold books of poems about animals together with models of animals that children bring into class.

After the boys and girls have read many poems about animals, have them select a favorite. Drawn or cut-out pictures of animals can be pasted to cardboard and attached to sticks to make hand puppets. Children can work the puppets while reading their favorite poem about the animal of their choice.

A similar idea was carried out by a first-grade teacher in California. She used the theme "Fish for a Poem" and featured a fish mobile. The mobile contained several poems about fish. Underneath the mobile a fishbowl with two goldfish was placed on a box. A second box was gaily decorated and contained poems about fish and the sea, which had been mounted on pieces of cardboard. A small hole was punched in each piece of cardboard, through which a paper clip was slipped. Children could take their "fishing poles"—long sticks with magnets attached to the ends—and literally fish for poetry.

Poetry Face to Face A mirror can be used to help introduce a variety of poems. Attach one to a bulletin board or hang one on a wall; around it place several poems about one's face or oneself. Near the mirror place several volumes of poetry. Poems might include "Robert, Who Is a Stranger to Himself" by Gwendolyn Brooks in *Bronzeville Boys and Girls*, or Carl Sandburg's "Phizzog" in *Rainbows Are Made: Poems by Carl Sandburg*, selected by me. The display might also contain pictures of the children in the class or baby pictures for peers to guess who *was* who!

Poetry Happenings A group of children can plan poetry happenings or dramatic readings of several poems relating to a specific subject. Poems can tie in with curriculum, specific interests such as sports or hobbies, or a subject—rocks, the city, famous people, or music. When they have a final selection, they can present a poetry happening for the class and for other classes in the school. To enhance the happening, simple props or creative dramatics can be employed.

Recently, I was invited to an elementary school in Westchester County, New York, where a group of fourth-graders presented a lavish production based on my collection *A Dog's Life.* The children wore masks they had made depicting various breeds of dogs. The simple staging on stools and ladders was enhanced by spotlights. One group taped sounds of dogs barking and howling for background effects; another group set Karla Kuskin's "Full of the Moon," which is included in the collection, to music. To see and hear nine-year-olds perform works by Carl Sandburg, Robert Frost, Harry Behn, and Gwendolyn Brooks was pure magic. The tender "For Mugs" by Myra Cohn Livingston, about a dog who has just died, brought chills to the entire audience.

Any grouping of poems lends itself to a multitude of production ideas. Try it!

A Poetry Jar An elementary teacher in Las Vegas, Nevada, devised a clever way to motivate her students to read poetry. A clear glass jar becomes the Poetry Jar. At the beginning of each week an object is placed in the jar.

Children then become poem hunters, seeking poetry that mentions or describes the object.

Objects might be toy models of cars or animals, realia such as a leaf, rock, or flower, or sometimes a live specimen such as an ant or a guppy. A larger container such as a fish tank might feature turtles, horned toads, or interesting fish.

Alongside the jar or tank leave a pencil and a pad of paper for those who want to sit, observe, and create poetry. The girls and boys might also try creating a variety of short verse forms based on the objects in the Poetry Jar.

A Poetry Weather Calendar Younger boys and girls will enjoy a poetry weather calendar. Use a large piece of oaktag for each month. List the month, weeks, and days of the week, along with the question "What is the weather like today?"

On the bottom of the chart attach several large brown envelopes labeled "Sun Poems," "Wind Poems," "Cloud Poems," "Rain Poems," or "Snow Poems." Collected poems can be placed within appropriate envelopes, which can be added to and used year after year. When the month, date, and day of the week have been discussed, a child can volunteer to tell what the weather is like, then choose an appropriate poem from an envelope to read or have read to the class. Weather combinations, such as "sunny and windy," can also be used.

Girls and boys can be encouraged to add to the envelopes as they find various weather poems throughout the year.

An excellent resource to use is Maurice Sendak's *Chicken Soup with Rice*, wherein the acclaimed author/illustrator sings praises of his favorite soup in gay themes and pictures for each month of the year. *Chicken Soup with Rice* is also available as a filmstrip set from Weston Woods, and as a book and cassette package from Scholastic, Inc.

Other sources to seek out include the section "Sun and Rain and Wind and Storms," in Myra Cohn Livingston's *A Song I Sang to You*; the section "Weather and Seasons" in Eve Merriam's *Jamboree*; the section "Rain, Sun, and Snow" in *Surprises*, selected by me; and Part 3, "I like it when it's mizzly . . . and just a little drizzly . . ." in Nancy Larrick's *Piping Down the Valleys Wild.*

Prose and Poetry Prose and poetry go well together. After children have read a favorite book or listened to one read aloud, follow it up with a poem.

Story hours provide wonderful opportunities to introduce poetry. After reading a book to students, follow with a poem that has the same theme. For example, if you read a book such as *The Snowy Day* by Ezra Jack Keats, you can add depth to the moment with a poem such as "Cynthia in the Snow" by Gwendolyn Brooks, in *Bronzeville Boys and Girls.* This enables children to hear a Caldecott Award–winning volume and a Pulitzer Prize–winning poet—all tucked into a ten- or fifteen-minute time period.

Older students can combine poetry with other forms of literature, too. After they have finished reading a novel, ask them to find a poem that reflects the book's subject or theme. For instance, after reading a Marguerite Henry or Walter Farley novel about horses, have them look for a poem about horses. A story such as *The Mouse and the Motorcycle* by Beverly Cleary is sure to send all those who like rodents scurrying for a poem that expresses feelings about mice.

Nonfiction can be dealt with in the same way. After boys and girls have read a book about dinosaurs, for example, have them look for a dinosaur poem to share.

Dinosaurs features poems about the beasts of yore, by poets such as Patricia Hubbell, Myra Cohn Livingston, Lilian Moore, and Valerie Worth, selected by me.

Misha Arenstein, a fourth-grade teacher in Scarsdale, New York, uses this technique for book-sharing: He has students tuck a poem related to a book inside the cover so that when others read it they already have a poem on hand to read, too. He then encourages readers to add another poem. Within months, one novel might have three, four, or more verses relating to the plot, characters, or setting inside the cover for this and future classes to enjoy.

Another idea to spark the use of poetry with prose is by having children read or re-read favorite fairy tales and introduce them to humorous verses about characters, plots, or situations. For example, after discussing the plot of "Cinderella," children will enjoy hearing such verse as ". . . And Then the Prince Knelt Down and Tried to Put the Glass Slipper on Cinderella's Foot" by Judith

Viorst in *If I Were in Charge of the World and Other Worries*, briefly relating how Cinderella has changed her mind about the handsome prince the day after the ball; the untitled verse encouraging Cinderella to *use* her wits which begins "Look Cinderella" in *A Song I Sang to You* by Myra Cohn Livingston; and the irreverent "Cinderella" in Roald Dahl's *Revolting Rhymes.*

Season Songs Scientists have set approximate dates for the arrival of each season in the Northern Hemisphere: autumn, September 21; winter, December 21; spring, March 21; summer, June 21. Check the correct dates and times in your local newspaper. The summer and winter dates, marking the days of longest and shortest daylight, are called "solstices." Spring and autumn occur when the sun is directly over the equator; these times are called equinoxes.

Mark the arrival of each season by taking the class on a neighborhood field trip. Let students look for the first signs of the season and perhaps collect some materials for a science table display. Time might also be set aside for some brainstorming in which students list words to describe the coming season. The words can be copied and/or mimeographed for each child to have and to use in writing his or her experiences.

Poetry reflecting the various seasons is abundant. For younger readers you might use *The Sky Is Full of Song*, selected by me, which contains thirty-eight poems celebrating the seasons.

Middle-graders will enjoy any of the five following titles:

Barbara Juster Esbensen's *Cold Stars and Fireflies* is a sparkling collection of forty-three original poems about nature and the changing seasons, with evocative illustrations touched with reds and grays.

Myra Cohn Livingston's *A Circle of Seasons* is an original thirteen-stanza poem following the cycle of the seasons.

Two anthologies include *Moments*, selected by me, containing fifty selections; Part 6, "I wonder what the spring will shout . . . ," in Nancy Larrick's *Piping Down the Valleys Wild* includes seventeen verses hailing the season.

Aileen Fisher's *Out in the Dark and Daylight* provides an abundance of original verses about the year and its many seasonal moods.

For additional references see "Poems to Celebrate" (pages 197–99), and "Poet of the Month" (pages 199–200).

See the Sea in Poetry A Las Vegas, Nevada, teacher uses a tabletop display entitled "Our Home—The Sea" to tie poetry into science, art, and literature. She covers a table with sand, a variety of seashells, and starfish. The display also contains a toy shovel and pail, which serves as a container for sea poems the students in her class find or write. Behind the display she places prints of great seascape paintings to further motivate youngsters to look at, feel, and write their own thoughts about the sea.

Sea Songs, a collection of original poems by Myra Cohn

Livingston, can be displayed, along with three anthologies: *The Ice-Cream Ocean and Other Delectable Poems of the Sea*, selected and illustrated by Susan Russo; *The Sea Is Calling Me*; and Section 5 of *Rainbows Are Made: Poems by Carl Sandburg*, both selected by me.

Once boys and girls have been exposed to various poets' work, they can be further encouraged to create original verse. The children's creations can be placed in the pail on the display. At the end of a given time both the poems the students found and the ones they themselves created can be bound into a scrapbook and illustrated with original drawing or pictures clipped from magazines and newspapers.

The Senses and Poetry Children can be sparked to create poems after they have had a variety of planned sensory experiences. One way to motivate boys and girls to use their senses is to take them for several walks around the neighborhood. Be specific on each walk. Tell the class, "Today we are going on a *hearing* walk to record only the various sounds we hear." On a second walk, children can record all that they see; on a third, all that they smell, and so on. During each walk the class can record all the various sounds they hear, sights they see, and so forth in a notebook.

A second-grade class went to visit a nearby pond for a "seeing" walk. The children saw many things but were fascinated by the many seed pods that appeared on the bank. After bringing the pods back into the classroom, several boys and girls wrote the following:

Seed pods when they break look like bombs exploding.

Seed pods sail like parachutes when they open.

The pods look like cotton candy when they are put together.

I could eat it, but I won't.

After several such walking trips, plans can be made for a sensory field trip. Visit an area the children have never seen before; a trip to a museum or a bakery, or even a ride on a train or merry-go-round, can produce excellent results when boys and girls are offered the opportunity to open up their senses.

A third-grade teacher in Indianapolis, Indiana, has her class listen to nature by providing them with imaginative questions. She asks: "How does a brook sound?" "What song does a cricket sing?" "What tool do you think of when you hear a woodpecker?" "How do raindrops sound against your umbrella?" "You are on a buffalo hunt with Indian friends. What sounds do you hear as the herd draws near?"

Such questions are good ones to ask before taking the class on a walking trip.

Sounds can arouse young writers. Another idea to inspire writing is to record or have students record a variety of sounds—bacon frying, the ticking of a clock, a slamming door, a baby crying, a typewriter or electric razor in action. After discussing sounds and noises and actually hearing them, a fourth-grade class in Harlem composed the following:

NOISE

Noise, noise everywhere
What to do! It's always there.
Bang! Pow! Zoom! Crunch!
Buzz! Crack! Crack! Munch!

In the air, on the ground,
Noise, noise all around.
Dogs barking, cars parking,
Planes flying, babies crying.

Sh . . . sh . . . time for sleep.
Not a single little peep.
Oh no—through the door—
Comes a noisy, awful snore.

Tick-tock—stop the clock.
Stop the yelling on my block.
Close the windows, shut them tight.
Cotton in ear—nighty-night.

Suzanne Hunsucker, a teacher at the Riverton High School in Wyoming, offered this idea for "sensational writing":

I bombarded [the children's] senses as they walked into the classroom . . . music was playing, crepe paper hanging. I passed out chocolate kisses and small pieces of material to feel, and I sprayed the air with spice room deodorizer. All this launched a good discussion of the senses. . . .

To develop the sense of touch, we blindfolded some volunteers and had them describe objects they were feeling without actually naming them. For sound, we wrote thoughts to music and tape recorded sounds. For development of sight, I first prepared a slide show of famous paintings and described how to look for such elements as shape, design, perspective, texture, movement, lighting, and color. Students began to really look at and analyze these works with a critical eye . . .

Nancy Larrick suggests additional ways to involve children in the sensory approach to writing poetry:

> Often it helps to bring in familiar objects which children can handle and then record their thoughts about . . . anything small enough to pick up and see from every angle. One group of fifth-graders soon set up what they called a "junk tray" from which they chose the inspiration for poetic images, even short poems . . .

In another class, wire coat hangers were twisted into modern sculpture, which led to poetry writing.

After children have had such sensory experiences, they can be encouraged to look for poems that deal with the senses and, of course, write their own verse.

Sing a Poem Music and poetry! Isn't that the perfect combination?

Several excellent collections of poems set to music get students singing, playing musical instruments, or experimenting with musical forms.

Lullabies and Night Songs, edited by William Engvick, with music by Alec Wilder and magnificent, full-color illustrations by Maurice Sendak, is as perfect now as when it first appeared in 1965. Forty-eight melodies appear in this oversized volume, including many Mother Goose rhymes and such gems as James Thurber's "The Golux's Song," Lewis Carroll's "The Crocodile," William Blake's "Cradle Song," and Robert Louis Stevenson's "Windy Night." A recording of the book, performed by Jan DeGaetani, is available from Caedmon.

Wonderland can be made a wee more wondrous with Lewis Carroll's *Songs from Alice.* Nine songs from *Alice's Adventures in Wonderland*, and ten from *Through the Looking Glass, and What Alice Found There*, are set for piano, guitar, and additional parts for violin, flute, or recorder. "Father William," "Turtle Soup," and "Jabberwocky" are among the familiar Lewis Carroll classics.

A handsome, eighty-page symphony, *The Moon on the One Hand* by William Crofut, with arrangements by Kenneth Cooper and Glen Shattuck, contains fifteen poems, most about nature and animals and including delights such as "in Just-" by E. E. Cummings; "The Chipmunk's Day," "The Mockingbird," and "Bird of the Night" by Randall Jarrell; and "Eletelephony" by Laura E. Richards. Arrangements include a variety of styles and instrumental possibilities—from piano to flute or the human voice.

Volumes such as these will lead students to set other poems to music, either those found in books or ones they have composed.

They can also be used to stage a classroom or assembly poetry musicale.

Sports in Poetry A sixth-grade teacher whets his students' poetry appetites with a sports in poetry bulletin board display.

A photo montage about a specific sport (baseball, football, water skiing), along with several related sports poems, is created by students. On the bulletin board is the following suggestion: "Make a photo montage about a sport you like. Find a poem about the sport. Or write one yourself."

Underneath the bulletin board is a tabletop display of books containing sports poems. Resources include two original books of verse by Lillian Morrison, *The Sidewalk Racer and Other Poems of Sports and Motion* and *The Break Dance Kids.* An anthology of poems selected by Lillian Morrison is *Sprints and Distances.*

Arnold Adoff's *Sports Pages* reflects the experiences and feelings of young athletes involved in various sports.

Styrofoam and Space Projects A study of space can tie in with current events and humankind explorations while presenting some excellent poetry. After the children have heard, read, or written poems about space, encourage them to do a display. Give the children small Styrofoam balls that they can paint with tempera paint. Next, provide them with round, colored toothpicks that can be inserted into the Styrofoam. Finished projects can be attached to a bulletin-board display featuring poems, current events clippings from newspapers and magazines, and students' original artwork. Several of the balls might be strung together to create hanging mobiles.

Poems About Outer Space is a boxed set, which I designed, that includes paperbound anthologies, eight spiritmaster activity sheets, four posters, and "I Love Poetry" stickers. A teachers' guide offers many further ideas to rocket your children into a study of outer space. The kit is available from Sundance Distributors.

What Is Poetry?

In addition to the many quotes about poetry that appear throughout the volume, here are some others that can be used as bulletin board sparklers for a variety of occasions or shared with students to evoke discussion:

Poetry is the most effective way of saying things. —Matthew Arnold

You may not shout when you remember poems you have read or learned, but you will know from your toes to your head that something has hit you. —Arna Bontemps

One of the skills of a good poet is to enact experiences rather than to talk about having had them. "*Show* it, don't *tell* it," the poet says, "make it happen, don't talk about its happening." —John Ciardi

Poetry is beautiful shorthand. —William Cole

A lot of people think or believe or know they feel—but that's thinking or believing or knowing; not feeling. And poetry is feeling—not knowing or believing or thinking. —E. E. Cummings

Poetry makes possible the deepest kind of personal possession of the world. —James Dickey

If I read a book and it makes my whole body so cold that no fire can ever warm me, I know that is poetry. If I feel physically as if the top of my head were taken *off*, I know that is poetry. These are the only ways I know it is. Is there another way? —Emily Dickinson

A poem . . . begins as a lump in the throat, a sense of wrong, a homesickness, a lovesickness. —Robert Frost

The basis of literary education is poetry. Poetry is rhythm, movement. The entering of poetic rhythm into the body of the reader is very important. It is something very close to the development of an athletic skill and, as such, it can't be rushed. —Northrop Frye

Poetry is comment on the world by people who see that world more clearly than other people and are moved by it. —Phyllis McGinley

Poetry is speaking painting. —Plutarch

Poetry is a sequence of dots and dashes, spelling depths, crypts, cross-lights, and moon-wisps. —Carl Sandburg

Poetry is a record of the best and happiest moments of the happiest and best minds. —Percy Bysshe Shelley

Poetry in Nonprint Media

This selected listing of audiovisual materials includes programs that have been used and enjoyed by a variety of educators and children to enhance poetic experiences. Items mentioned in other parts of this volume are not described again below.

Recordings *The* source to consult for recordings is *International Index to Recorded Poetry*, compiled by Herbert H. Hoffman and Rita L. Hoffman, a guide to over 1,700

phonodiscs, tapes, cassettes, and filmstrips. The compilers have attempted to include every poetry recording released through 1980, anywhere in the world, in any language. Some 2,300 poets are represented by about 15,000 poems, in more than twenty languages. The compendium is divided into six sections: author index, title index, first line index, reader index, a register of poets by language of composition, and a list of recordings analyzed.

Caedmon offers a variety of poetry recordings. *A Gathering of Great Poetry for Children*, edited by Richard Lewis, is a four-set package, featuring the work of contemporary and classic poets, ranging from A. A. Milne to Gwendolyn Brooks. Several poems are read by the poets themselves—Carl Sandburg, Robert Frost, T. S. Eliot; others are read by Julie Harris, Cyril Ritchard, and David Wayne.

Caedmon has also produced *Silver Pennies* and *More Silver Pennies*, a two-record set narrated by Claire Bloom and Cyril Ritchard, containing selections from the books of the same title, edited by Blanche Jennings Thompson, published in 1925 and 1930. Many poems in the first album deal with fantasy and imaginative creatures—fairies, elves, goblins; the second album examines people's feelings and values.

Filmstrip Sets Guidance Associates features *A Pocketful of Poetry*, a set of two filmstrips and cassettes, designed to introduce children to writing poetry, and *Poems for Glad, Poems for Sad*, two filmstrips and cassettes dealing with emotions.

Mature students can be introduced to classic poets and poetry via nine filmstrip sets in the *Living Poetry* series, produced by McGraw-Hill. Original artwork and music enhance dramatic readings, encouraging students to read the original verses. Titles in the series include "Hiawatha's Childhood," part 3 of Henry Wadsworth Longfellow's twenty-two-part *The Song of Hiawatha*, which begins after the birth of Hiawatha, continuing to his entrance into manhood; "The Deacon's Masterpiece," Oliver Wendell Holmes' poem about the "one-hoss shay . . . it ran a hundred years to a day"; "Casey at the Bat" by Ernest Lawrence Thayer, which depicts the excitement and tension of the Mudville nine's valiant try for victory in the bottom of the ninth, with two away, two men on, and the mighty Casey coming to bat; *Poems of Lewis Carroll*, featuring three poems, "Father William," "The Walrus and the Carpenter," and "The Gardener's Song"; "Paul Revere's Ride" by Henry Wadsworth Longfellow, which captures the urgency and magnitude of Revere's mission when "the fate of a nation was riding that night . . ."; *Poems of Tennyson and Browning*, including Robert Browning's "Incident of the French Camp" and Tennyson's "The Charge of the Light Brigade," along with a guide providing brief historical backgrounds to the incidents on which the poems were based; *Poems by Walt Whitman*, featuring "I Hear America Singing," "Miracles," "When I Heard the Learn'd Astronomer," and "O Captain! My Captain!"

Random House has produced *Pick a Peck o' Poems*, six filmstrip sets that I edited featuring poems by contemporary poets that are woven into a narrative, defining poetic terms in simple language. *What Is Poetry?* introduces rhyme, free verse, and imagery, showing similarities and differences; *Sing a Song of Cities* features poems about how people travel, shop, play, and build on city streets; *Animals, Animals, Animals* includes poems about pets in houses, jungles, zoos, and museums; *When It's Cold, and When It's Not* depicts weather and the four seasons; *Our Earth to Keep* is a plea for keeping the earth beautiful; *A Poem Belongs to You* encourages writing poetry. Included is a teacher's guide with reprints of the poems heard on the recordings.

Also from Random House is Nancy Willard's *A Visit to William Blake's Inn: Poems for Innocent and Experienced Travelers*, a filmstrip set based on the author's 1982 Newbery Award–winning volume. Using the Caldecott Honor Book illustrations by Alice and Martin Provensen, this adaptation further enhances the mood of the verse with the addition of a musical score. A complement to the set is the filmstrip *Meet the Newbery Author: Nancy Willard.*

SVE's four-filmstrip set portrays *Animals in Verse.* Titles include "Animal Mothers and Babies," "Animals in the City," "Animals in the Zoo," and "Animals on the Farm." Outstanding photography and original music and lyrics highlight the presentations; a teacher's guide is included.

Also from SVE is *Seasons of Poetry*, a set of four filmstrips depicting the changing seasons; a teacher's guide is included.

Professional Cassettes In *Take a Poetry Break: Making Poetry Come Alive for Children*, produced by the American Library Association and distributed by PBS Video, Caroline Feller Bauer addresses a group of educators, quickly dispelling the myth that poetry is dull or boring. She talks about some of America's top poets for children and presents a host of ideas meshing poetry and media.

Tapping into children's interests in such topics as animals, food, humor, and money, she demonstrates how poetry can enhance every area of the curriculum. The cassette is perfect to share at faculty meetings, at in-service programs, or with parent groups. Write to PBS Video for costs of buying and/or renting the cassette.

Also consult Ms. Bauer's professional books, *This Way to Books* and *Celebrations*, for further ideas on presenting poetry.

REFERENCES

Adler, David A. *You Think It's Fun to Be a Clown!* Illustrated by Ray Cruz. Doubleday, 1980.

Adoff, Arnold. *Eats: Poems.* Illustrated by Susan Russo. Lothrop, Lee & Shepard, 1979.

———. *Sports Pages.* Illustrated by Steve Kuzma. J. B. Lippincott, 1986.

Bauer, Caroline Feller. *Celebrations.* H. W. Wilson, 1985.

———. *This Way to Books.* H. W. Wilson, 1982.

Benét, Rosemary, and Benét, Stephen Vincent. *A Book of Americans.* Illustrated by Charles Child. Henry Holt, 1933, 1961.

Brewton, John E.; Blackburn, Lorraine A.; and Blackburn, George M. III (compilers). *In the Witch's Kitchen: Poems for Halloween.* Illustrated by Harriet Brown. T. Y. Crowell, 1980.

Brewton, Sara, and Brewton, John E. (compilers). *Shrieks at Midnight.* Illustrated by Ellen Raskin. T. Y. Crowell, 1969.

Brooks, Gwendolyn. *Bronzeville Boys and Girls.* Illustrated by Ronni Solbert. Harper & Row, 1956.

Carroll, Lewis. *Songs from Alice.* Music by Don Harper. Illustrated by Charles Folkard. Holiday House, 1979.

Cole, William (compiler). *Good Dog Poems.* Illustrated by Ruth Sanderson. Scribner's, 1981.

———. *Poem Stew.* Illustrated by Karen Ann Weinhaus. J. B. Lippincott, 1981; also in paperback.

———. *Poetry of Horses.* Illustrated by Ruth Sanderson. Scribner's, 1979.

Cleary, Beverly. *The Mouse and the Motorcyle.* Illustrated by Louis Darling. William Morrow, 1965; Dell paperback.

Crofut, William. *The Moon on the One Hand: Poetry in Song.* Arrangements by Kenneth Cooper and Glenn Shattuck. Illustrated by Susan Crofut. Atheneum, 1975.

Dahl, Roald. *Revolting Rhymes.* Illustrated by Quentin Blake. Alfred A. Knopf, 1982.

de Regniers, Beatrice Schenk. *So Many Cats.* Illustrated by Ellen Weiss. Clarion, 1986.

———. *Something Special.* Illustrated by Irene Haas. Harcourt Brace Jovanovich, 1958.

———. *This Big Cat and Other Cats I've Known.* Illustrated by Alan Daniel. Crown, 1985.

Eliot, T. S. *Old Possum's Book of Practical Cats.* Illustrated by Edward Gorey. Harcourt Brace Jovanovich, 1982; revised edition; also in paperback.

Engvick, William (editor). *Lullabies and Night Songs.* Music by Alec Wilder. Illustrated by Maurice Sendak. Harper & Row, 1965.

Esbensen, Barbara Juster. *Cold Stars and Fireflies: Poems of the Four Seasons.* Illustrated by Susan Bonners. T. Y. Crowell, 1984.

Fisher, Aileen. *Out in the Dark and Daylight.* Illustrated by Gail Owens. Harper & Row, 1980.

Hoffman, Herbert H., and Hoffman, Rita L. *International Index to Recorded Poetry.* H. W. Wilson, 1983.

Hopkins, Lee Bennett (selector). *Beat the Drum! Independence Day Has Come.* Illustrated by Tomie de Paola. Harcourt Brace Jovanovich, 1977.

———. *Creatures.* Illustrated by Stella Ormai. Harcourt Brace Jovanovich, 1985.

———. *Dinosaurs.* Illustrated by Murray Tinkleman. Harcourt Brace Jovanovich, 1987.

———. *A Dog's Life.* Illustrated by Linda Rochester Richards. Harcourt Brace Jovanovich, 1983.

———. *Easter Buds Are Springing.* Illustrated by Tomie de Paola. Harcourt Brace Jovanovich, 1970.

———. *Good Morning to You, Valentine.* Illustrated by Tomie de Paola. Harcourt Brace Jovanovich, 1976.

———. *Hey-How for Halloween.* Illustrated by Janet McCaffery. Harcourt Brace Jovanovich, 1974.

———. *I Am the Cat.* Illustrated by Linda Rochester Richards. Harcourt Brace Jovanovich, 1982.

———. *Merrily Comes Our Harvest In: Poems for Thanksgiving.* Illustrated by Ben Shecter. Harcourt Brace Jovanovich, 1978.

———. *Moments: Poems About the Seasons.* Illustrated by Michael Hague. Harcourt Brace Jovanovich, 1980.

———. *Munching: Poems About Eating.* Illustrated by Nelle Davis. Little, Brown, 1985.

———. *My Mane Catches the Wind: Poems About Horses.* Illustrated by Sam Savitt. Harcourt Brace Jovanovich, 1979.

———. *Rainbows Are Made: Poems by Carl Sandburg.* Illustrated by Fritz Eichenberg. Harcourt Brace Jovanovich, 1982; also in paperback.

———. *The Sea Is Calling Me.* Illustrated by Walter Gaffney-Kessell. Harcourt Brace Jovanovich, 1986.

———. *Sing Hey for Christmas Day.* Illustrated by Laura Jean Allen. Harcourt Brace Jovanovich, 1975.

———. *The Sky Is Full of Song.* Illustrated by Dirk Zimmer. Harper & Row, 1983; also in paperback.

———. *A Song in Stone.* Illustrated by Anna Held Audette. T. Y. Crowell, 1983.

———. *Surprises.* An I Can Read Book. Illustrated by Megan Lloyd. Harper & Row, 1983; also in paperback.

Hughes, Langston. *Selected Poems.* Illustrated by E. McKnight Kauffer. Alfred A. Knopf, 1966.

Keats, Ezra Jack. *The Snowy Day.* Viking, 1962; also in paperback.

Kuskin, Karla. *Dogs & Dragons, Trees & Dreams: A Collection of Poems.* Harper & Row, 1980.

Larrick, Nancy (selector). *Crazy to Be Alive in Such a Strange World: Poems About People.* M. Evans, 1979.

———. *Piping Down the Valleys Wild.* Illustrated by Ellen Raskin. Doubleday, 1985; revised edition; Dell paperback.

Livingston, Myra Cohn. *Celebrations.* Illustrated by Leonard Everett Fisher. Holiday House, 1985.

———. *A Circle of Seasons.* Illustrated by Leonard Everett Fisher. Holiday House, 1982.

———. *Sea Songs.* Illustrated by Leonard Everett Fisher. Holiday House, 1985.

———. *A Song I Sang to You.* Illustrated by Margot Tomes. Harcourt Brace Jovanovich, 1984.

——— (selector). *Callooh! Callay! Holiday Poems for Young Readers.* Illustrated by Janet Stevens. Margaret K. McElderry Books/Macmillan, 1978.

———. *Christmas Poems.* Illustrated by Trina Schart Hyman. Holiday House, 1984.

———. *Easter Poems.* Illustrated by John Wallner. Holiday House, 1985.

———. *O Frabjous Day! Poetry for Holidays and Special Occasions.* Margaret K. McElderry Books/Macmillan, 1977.

———. *Poems for Jewish Holidays.* Illustrated by Lloyd Bloom. Holiday House, 1986.

———. *Poems of Christmas.* Margaret K. McElderry Books/Macmillan, 1980.

———. *Thanksgiving Poems.* Illustrated by Stephen Gammel. Holiday House, 1985.

———. *Why Am I Grown So Cold? Poems of the Unknowable.* Margaret K. McElderry Books/Macmillan, 1982.

Merriam, Eve. *Jamboree: Rhymes for All Times.* Illustrated by Walter Gaffney-Kessell. Dell paperback, 1984.

Moore, Lilian. *Something New Begins: New and Selected Poems.* Atheneum, 1982.

Moore, Vardine. *Mice Are Rather Nice: Poems About Mice.* Illustrated by Doug Jamison. Atheneum, 1981.

Morrison, Lillian. *The Break Dance Kids: Poems of Sport, Motion and Locomotion.* Lothrop, 1985.

———. *The Sidewalk Racer and Other Poems of Sports and Motion.* Lothrop, Lee & Shepard, 1977.

——— (selector). *Sprints and Distances: Sports in Poetry and Poetry in Sports.* Illustrated by Clare and John Ross. T. Y. Crowell, 1965.

O'Neill, Mary. *Hailstones and Halibut Bones: Adventures in Color.* Illustrated by Leonard Weisgard. Doubleday, 1961.

Pellowski, Anne; Sattley, Helen R.; and Arkhurst, Joyce C. *Have You Seen a Comet? Children's Art and Writing from Around the World.* John Day, 1971.

Prelutsky, Jack. *Circus.* Illustrated by Arnold Lobel. Macmillan, 1974; also in paperback.

———. *The Headless Horseman Rides Tonight: More Poems to Trouble Your Sleep.* Illustrated by Arnold Lobel. Greenwillow, 1980.

———. *It's Christmas.* Illustrated by Marylin Hafner. Greenwillow, 1981.

———. *It's Halloween.* Illustrated by Marylin Hafner. Greenwillow, 1977; also in Scholastic paperback.

———. *It's Thanksgiving.* Illustrated by Marylin Hafner. Greenwillow, 1982; also in Scholastic paperback.

———. *It's Valentine's Day.* Illustrated by Yossi Abolafia. Greenwillow, 1983; also in Scholastic paperback.

———. *Nightmares: Poems to Trouble Your Sleep.* Illustrated by Arnold Lobel. Greenwillow, 1976.

Russo, Susan (selector). *The Ice-Cream Ocean and Other Delectable Poems of the Sea.* Lothrop, 1984.

Sendak, Maurice. *Chicken Soup with Rice: A Book of Months.* Harper & Row, 1962; also in paperback.

Seuss, Dr. *If I Ran the Circus.* Random House, 1956; also in paperback.

Silverstein, Shel. *Where the Sidewalk Ends.* Harper & Row, 1974.

Viorst, Judith. *If I Were in Charge of the World and Other Worries.* Illustrated by Lynne Cherry. Atheneum, 1981; also in paperback.

Wyndham, Robert (editor). *Chinese Mother Goose Rhymes.* Illustrated by Ed Young. Putnam, 1982; also in paperback.

A Brief Afterword

In A. A. Milne's delightful classic *The House at Pooh Corner* (Dutton, 1928), the renowned Winnie-the-Pooh sums up the creation of poetry in one line. He tells his friend Piglet, "It is the best way to write poetry, letting things come."

Letting things come is the way of poetry, for poetry can help life along no matter what age or stage of development we are at:

Poetry can—

Make you chuckle,
or laugh, or cry,
make you dance
or shout, or sigh.

Why? Because poetry, like life, comes about naturally. For each step we take, each decade we live, poetry can weave

in and out
  and
up and down
  and
around and around
us—just like life itself.

Letting things come, letting poetry come into the lives of children, is one of the best things any of us can do as adults. And we can help by taking the poetic advice of Beatrice Schenk de Regniers when she tells us to "keep a poem in your pocket" (see page 56).

So—*keep* a poem in your pocket—or pocketbook, or briefcase, or shopping bag. Pull it out when needed or wanted and spread it around freely. In short—pass the poetry—*please!*

Appendixes

Appendix 1
Poetry Reflecting Contemporary Issues

Two important contemporary subjects for today's child are the city and multi-ethnic experiences.

This selected list cites some of the best collections of original poems and anthologies containing poems about these topics.

The City

Brooks, Gwendolyn. *Bronzeville Boys and Girls.* Illustrated by Ronni Solbert. Harper & Row, 1956. See pages 41–44.

Hopkins, Lee Bennett (selector). *A Song in Stone: City Poems.* Illustrated by Anna Held Audette. T. Y. Crowell, 1982.

This American Library Association Notable Book of 1983 features twenty selections, including works by Patricia Hubbell, Judith Thurman, and Norma Farber, illustrated with black-and-white photographs.

Janeczko, Paul (editor). *Postcard Poems: A Collection for Sharing.* Bradbury Press, 1973.

Several city images appear in this volume of 109 poems for mature readers such as "On Watching the Construction of a Skyscraper" by Burton Raffel, "Street Windows" by Carl Sandburg, and "Blue Alert" by Eve Merriam.

Kennedy, X. J. *The Forgetful Wishing Well: Poems for Young People.* Illustrated by Monica Incisa. Margaret K. McElderry Books, 1985.

Part 6 of this volume, "In the City," contains eight selections including "Boulder, Colorado," "Forty-Seventh Street Crash," and "Flying Uptown Backwards."

Larrick, Nancy (editor). *Piping Down the Valleys Wild.* Illustrated by Ellen Raskin. Delacorte, reissued 1985; also in paperback.

Part 14, "The City Spreads Its Wings," from Langston Hughes' poem "City," contains eleven poems such as "Mrs. Peck-Pigeon" by Eleanor Farjeon, "Concrete Mixers" by Patricia Hubbell, and "City Lights" by Rachel Field.

Moore, Lilian (selector). *Go with the Poem: A New Collection.* McGraw-Hill, 1979.

Part 6, "The City: We Call It Home," contains eleven selections, including "Rain" by Adrien Stoutenberg, "The Yawn" by Paul Blackburn, and "New York in the Spring" by David Budbill.

———. *Something New Begins.* Illustrated by Mary Jane Dunton. Atheneum, 1982.

Although not all of the selections in this volume are city-oriented, there are enough here to share, including such gems as "Pigeons," "Foghorns," and "Mural on Second Avenue." See also pages 19–20.

The Black Experience

This selected list cites volumes published between 1956 and the present. Although the poems are mainly geared toward mature readers, you will find some within the volumes that can be used with younger children.

Adoff, Arnold.

For titles of Mr. Adoff's books dealing with black and multiracial experiences, see pages 27–31.

Brooks, Gwendolyn. *Bronzeville Boys and Girls.* Illustrated by Ronni Solbert. Harper & Row, 1956. See pages 41–44.

Bryan, Ashley (selector). *I Greet the Dawn: Poems by Paul Laurence Dunbar.* Atheneum, 1978.

Following a brief introduction of Paul Laurence Dunbar (1872–1906) and his work, Mr. Bryan presents six sections of the poet's work. Although much of the poet's work was written in dialect, such as these first lines from "Little Brown Baby":

> Little brown baby wif spa'klin eyes,
> Come to yo' pappy an' set on his knee . . .

Mr. Bryan has selected poems in standard English, leaving in a few dialect poems. The volume is illustrated with black-and-white drawings by the compiler.

Clifton, Lucille. See pages 53–55.

Giovanni, Nikki. See pages 74–77.

Greenfield, Eloise. *Honey, I Love and Other Love Poems.* Illustrated by Leo and Diane Dillon. T. Y. Crowell, 1978; also available in paperback.

Fifteen poems appear in a small-size format with delightful illustrations. Excerpts from the book appear on the recording of the same title (Caedmon), performed by the author and friends and enhanced by a lively jazz accompaniment.

Hughes, Langston. See pages 79–83.

McKissack, Patricia C. *Paul Laurence Dunbar: A Poet to Remember.* Children's Press, 1984.

A biography of the poet for mature readers.

American Indians and Eskimos

Bierhorst, John (editor). *In the Trails of the Wind: American Indian Poems and Ritual Orations.* Farrar, Straus & Giroux, 1971.

Translated from over forty languages, this collection of 126 poems represents the best-known Indian cultures of North and South America. Omens, battle songs, orations, love lyrics, prayers, dreams, and mystical incantations are included, beginning with the origin of the earth and the emergence of humans through to the apocalyptic visions of a new life. Detailed notes appear on each of the selections along with suggestions for further reading and glossary of tribes, cultures, and languages, which give insight into the poetry. The volume is illustrated with black-and-white period engravings.

———. *The Sacred Path: Spells, Prayers and Power Songs of the American Indians.* William Morrow, 1983.

As in the above title, this volume draws upon classic sources, representing the many cultures of North, South, and Central America, incorporating material unavailable until the 1970s and 1980s. The anthology is arranged as a progression—from "Birth and Infancy" to "For the Dying and the Dead." Selections used in rituals by such tribes as the Cherokee, Aztec, and Chippewa are associated with love, sickness, weather, farming, and hunting. Notes, sources, and a glossary of tribes, cultures, and languages are appended.

———. *Songs of the Chippewa.* Adapted from collections of Frances Densmore and Henry Rowe Schoolcraft and arranged for piano and guitar. Illustrated by Joe Servello. Farrar, Straus and Giroux, 1974.

Authoritatively edited and with the inclusion of lavish paintings, this volume contains seventeen chants, dream songs, medicine charms, and lullabies, collected near the western shores of the Great Lakes by Frances Densmore during the 1900s, and by Henry Rowe Schoolcraft more than one-half century earlier. An introduction and section of notes appear.

Jones, Hettie (compiler). *The Trees Stand Shining.* Illustrated by Robert Andrew Parker. Dial Press, 1971; also in paperback.

This volume will appeal to younger children because of its format—a large picture book containing beautiful full-color paintings. The anthologist arranged this collection to trace a journey through two days' time; she tells the reader that "the poems . . . are really songs. In their songs, American Indians told how they felt about the world, all they saw in the land, what they did in their lives." The songs are from such tribes as the Iroquois, Teton Sioux, Chippewa, and Papago.

Appendix 2

*Poetry in Paperback: A Selected List**

Ciardi, John. *Fast and Slow.* Illustrated by Becky Gaver. Houghton Mifflin.

Thirty-four early poems are featured in this volume of humorous and nonsense verse.

*———. *The Man Who Sang the Sillies.* J. B. Lippincott.

Cole, William. *A Boy Named Mary Jane and Other Silly Verse.* Illustrated by George MacClain. Avon.

Twenty-four original, humorous poems, including "Banananananananana," about a boy who loses the spelling bee because he cannot stop spelling "banana"; "Snorkeling," and "Piggy."

*———. *Poem Stew.* Harper & Row.

*de Angeli, Marguerite. *Book of Nursery Rhymes and Mother Goose Rhymes.* Doubleday.

deGasztold, Carmen Bernos. *Creature's Choir.* Illustrated by Jean Primrose. Viking.

Translated from the French by Rumer Godden, this volume includes poems about various animals, such as "The Snail," "The Centipede," "The Whale," and "The Fly."

———. *Prayers from the Ark.* Illustrated by Jean Primrose. Viking.

Translated from the French by Rumer Godden, this volume features prayers uttered by various animals—"The Prayer of the Little Ducks," "The Prayer of the Elephant," "The Prayer of the Little Pig."

Dickinson, Emily. *I'm Nobody! Who Are You? Poems of Emily Dickinson for Children.* Illustrated by Rex Schneider. Stemmer House.

---

*Titles marked with an asterisk are discussed within the the text of this volume.

Forty-five selections culled from the works of Emily Dickinson (1830–1866), including "There Is No Frigate Like a Book," "A Word Is Dead," and "Dear March, Come In."

*Eliot, T. S. *Old Possum's Book of Practical Cats.* Illustrated by Edward Gorey. Harcourt Brace Jovanovich.

*Frost, Robert. *A Swinger of Birches: Poems of Robert Frost for Young People.* Illustrated by Peter Koeppen. Stemmer House.

Greenfield, Eloise. *Honey, I Love and Other Love Poems.* Illustrated by Diane and Leo Dillon. Harper & Row.

*Hopkins, Lee Bennett (selector). *Rainbows Are Made: Poems by Carl Sandburg.* Illustrated by Fritz Eichenberg. Harcourt Brace Jovanovich.

*———. *The Sky Is Full of Song.* Illustrated by Dirk Zimmer. Harper & Row.

*———. *Surprises.* Illustrated by Megan Lloyd. Harper & Row.

*Jones, Hettie (selector). *The Trees Stand Shining.* Illustrated by Robert Andrew Parker. Dial.

*Larrick, Nancy (selector). *Piping Down the Valleys Wild.* Illustrated by Ellen Raskin. Dell.

*McCord, David. *All Small.* Illustrated by Madelaine Gill Linden. Little, Brown.

*———. *Every Time I Climb a Tree.* Illustrated by Marc Simont. Little, Brown.

Nash, Ogden. *Custard and Company.* Illustrated by Quentin Blake. Little, Brown.

Ogden Nash's nonsense verses are included, featuring eighty-four selections from the various published works of the poet, from the early 1930s through to the early 1960s.

*Merriam, Eve. *Jamboree: Rhymes for All Times.* Illustrated by Walter Gaffney-Kessell. Dell.

*———. *A Sky Full of Poems.* Illustrated by Walter Gaffney-Kessell. Dell.

*Prelutsky, Jack. *It's Halloween.* Illustrated by Marylin Hafner. Scholastic.

*———. *It's Thanksgiving.* Illustrated by Marylin Hafner. Scholastic.

*———. *It's Valentine's Day.* Illustrated by Yossi Abolafia. Scholastic.

*Sandburg, Carl. *Early Moon.* Illustrated by James Daugherty. Harcourt Brace Jovanovich.

*———. *Wind Song.* Illustrated by William A. Smith. Harcourt Brace Jovanovich.

Smith, William Jay. *Laughing Time: Nonsense Poems.* Illustrated by Fernando Krahn. Dell.

A host of humorous poems, perfect for reading aloud, is offered in this whimsical collection of light verse.

Viorst, Judith. *If I Were in Charge of the World and Other Worries.* Illustrated by Lynne Cherry. Atheneum.

Forty-one humorous verses appear with such titles as ". . . And Then the Prince Knelt Down and Tried to Put the Glass Slipper on Cinderella's Foot," and "Thoughts on Getting Out of a Nice Warm Bed in an Ice-Cold House to Go to the Bathroom at Three O'Clock in the Morning." The volume is divided into ten sections with headings such as "Fairy Tales," "Wicked Thoughts," and "Cats and Other People."

*Willard, Nancy. *A Visit to William Blake's Inn: Poems for Innocent and Experienced Travelers.* Illustrated by Alice and Martin Provensen. Harcourt Brace Jovanovich.

*Wyndham, Robert (selector). *Chinese Mother Goose Rhymes.* Illustrated by Ed Young. Putnam's.

Appendix 3

Sources of Educational Materials Cited

American Library Association, 50 E. Huron St., Chicago, IL 60611
Atheneum, 115 5th Ave., New York, NY 10003
Avon Books, 959 8th Ave., New York, NY 10019
Bradbury (see Macmillan)
Bobbs-Merrill, 4300 W. 62nd St., Indianapolis, IN 46206
Broadside Press, 12651 Old Mill Pl., Detroit, MI 48238
Caedmon, 1995 Broadway, New York, NY 10023
CBS Records, 51 W. 52nd St., New York, NY 10022
Children's Book Council, 67 Irving Pl., New York, NY 10003
Churchill Films, 662 N. Robertson Blvd., Los Angeles, CA 90069
Clarion Books, 52 Vanderbilt Ave., New York, NY 10017
T. Y. Crowell (see Harper & Row)
Crown, 225 Park Ave. S., New York, NY 10016
John Day, 257 Park Ave. S., New York, NY 10010
Delacorte, 245 E. 47th St., New York, NY 10017
Dell (see Delacorte)
Dial, 2 Park Ave., New York, NY 10016
Dodd, Mead, 79 Madison Ave., New York, NY 10016
Doubleday, 245 Park Ave., New York, NY 10017
Dutton (see Dial)
Earworks, Arnold Adoff Agency, Box 293, Yellow Springs, OH 45387
M. Evans, 216 E. 49th St., New York, NY 10017
Gale Research, Book Tower, Detroit, MI 48226
Garrard, 1607 N. Market St., Champaign, IL 61820
David Godine, 306 Dartmouth St., Boston, MA 02116
Greenwillow, 105 Madison Ave., New York, NY 10016
Guidance Associates, Pleasantville, NY 10570

Farrar, Straus & Giroux, 19 Union Square W., New York, NY 10003
Folkways Records, 43 W. 61st St., New York, NY 10023
Harcourt Brace Jovanovich, 1250 6th Ave., San Diego, CA 92101
Harper & Row, 10 E. 53rd St., New York, NY 10022
Hill, Lawrence (see Farrar, Straus & Giroux)
Hill and Wang (see Farrar, Straus & Giroux)
Holiday House, 18 E. 53rd St., New York, NY 10022
Henry Holt, 521 5th Ave., New York, NY 10175
Houghton Mifflin, 2 Park St., Boston, MA 02107
Alfred A. Knopf, 201 E. 50th St., New York, NY 10022
J. B. Lippincott (see Harper & Row)
Listening Library, 1 Park Ave., Old Greenwich, CT 06870
Little, Brown, 34 Beacon St., Boston, MA 02106
Lothrop, Lee & Shepard (see Greenwillow)
Macmillan, 866 3rd Ave., New York, NY 10022
McGraw-Hill, 1221 Ave. of the Americas, New York, NY 10020
William Morrow (see Greenwillow)
National Council of Teachers of English (NCTE), 1111 Kenyon Rd., Urbana, IL 61801
Oxford University Press, 200 Madison Ave., New York, NY 10016
Parachute Records, Inc., 8255 Sunset Blvd., Los Angeles, CA 90046
PBS Video, 475 L'Enfant Plaza, S.W., Washington, D.C. 20024
Pied Piper Productions, Box 320, Verdugo City, CA 91046
Clarkson M. Potter (see Crown)
Prentice-Hall, Englewood Cliffs, NJ 07632
G. P. Putnam's, 51 Madison Ave., New York, NY 10010
Random House (see Alfred A. Knopf)
Scholastic, Inc., 730 Broadway, New York, NY 10003
Scribner's (see Atheneum)
Simon and Schuster, 1230 Ave. of the Americas, New York, NY 10020
Spoken Arts, P.O. Box 289, New Rochelle, NY 10820
Stemmer House, 2626 Caves Rd., Owings Mills, MD 21117
SVE, 1345 Diversey Parkway, Chicago, IL 60614
Charles Tuttle, Rutland, VT 05701

United States Government Printing Office, Superintendent of Documents, Washington, D.C. 20401
Viking, 40 W. 23rd St., New York, NY 10010
Weston Woods, Weston, CT 06880
H. W. Wilson, 950 University Ave., Bronx, NY 10452
Zaner-Bloser, 2300 W. 5th Ave., P.O. Box 16764, Columbus, OH 43216.

Appendix 4
Mother Goose Collections

de Angeli, Marguerite. *Book of Nursery and Mother Goose Rhymes.* Doubleday, 1954; also in paperback.

This Caldecott Honor Book contains 376 rhymes, with over 260 full-color and black-and-white illustrations.

de Paola, Tomie. *Mother Goose.* Putnam's, 1985.

Over 200 Mother Goose rhymes illustrated with vibrant, full-color paintings.

———. *Mother Goose Story Streamers.* Putnam's, 1984.

This set of four streamers, perfect for bulletin-board displays, includes "Baa, Baa, Black Sheep," "Hey Diddle Diddle," "Jack and Jill," and "Little Miss Muffet."

Hague, Michael. *Mother Goose: A Collection of Classic Nursery Rhymes.* Holt, Rinehart & Winston, 1984.

Over forty-five rhymes illustrated in full color.

Lobel, Arnold. *Gregory Griggs and Other Nursery Rhyme People.* Greenwillow, 1978.

Thirty-four nursery rhymes about lesser-known but colorful ladies and gents such as "Hannah Bantry," "Terrance McDidler," and "Little Miss Tucket" (who sat on a bucket), each illustrated with lush, full-color drawings.

———. *The Random House Book of Mother Goose.* Random House, 1986.

Over 300 nursery rhymes selected and illustrated by the Caldecott Medalist.

Provensen, Alice and Martin. *The Mother Goose Book.* Random House, 1976.

More than 150 rhymes beautifully illustrated in full color.

Tripp, Wallace. *Granfa' Grig Had a Pig and Other Rhymes Without Reason from Mother Goose.* Little Brown, 1976; also in paperback.

This host of rhymes is whimsically illustrated in full color.

ACKNOWLEDGMENTS

Thanks are due to the following for the use of the copyrighted selections listed below:

Atheneum Publishers, Inc. for "New Day" from *Pigeon Cubes* by N. M. Bodecker. Copyright © 1982 N. M. Bodecker (A Margaret K. McElderry Book); "Blow-Up" from *The Forgetful Wishing Well* by X. J. Kennedy. Copyright © 1985 X. J. Kennedy (A Margaret K. McElderry Book); "Foghorns" from *I Thought I Heard the City* (1969) in the compilation *Something New Begins* by Lilian Moore. Copyright © 1982 by Lilian Moore. All reprinted with the permission of Atheneum Publishers, Inc.

Beatrice Schenk de Regniers for "Keep a Poem in Your Pocket" from *Something Special.* Copyright © 1958 by Beatrice Schenk de Regniers. Reprinted by permission of the author.

Harcourt Brace Jovanovich, Inc. for "Bubbles" from *Wind Song* by Carl Sandburg. Copyright © 1960 by Carl Sandburg. Reprinted by permission of Harcourt Brace Jovanovich, Inc.

Harper & Row, Publishers, Inc. for "Skipper" from *Bronzeville Boys and Girls* by Gwendolyn Brooks. Copyright © 1956 by Gwendolyn Brooks Blakely; "Out in the Dark and Daylight" from *Out in the Dark and Daylight* by Aileen Fisher. Copyright © 1980 by Aileen Fisher; "Hughbert and the Glue" from *Dogs & Dragons, Trees & Dreams: A Collection of Poems* by Karla Kuskin. Copyright © 1964 by Karla Kuskin; "The Search" from *Where the Sidewalk Ends: Poems and Drawings of Shel Silverstein.* Copyright © 1974 by Snake Eye Music, Inc.; "Mummy Slept Late and Daddy Fixed Breakfast" from *You Read to Me, I'll Read to You* by John Ciardi (J. B. Lippincott). Copyright © 1962 by John Ciardi; "Poetry" from *Eleanor Farjeon's Poems for Children* (J. B. Lippincott). Copyright © 1938, renewed 1966 by Eleanor Farjeon; first ten lines from *black is brown is tan* by Arnold Adoff. Copyright © 1973 by Arnold Adoff. All reprinted by permission of Harper & Row, Publishers, Inc.

ACKNOWLEDGMENTS

Henry Holt and Company, Inc. for the six-line excerpt from *Everett Anderson's Goodbye* by Lucille Clifton. Copyright © 1983 by Lucille Clifton; "The Pasture" from *The Poetry of Robert Frost,* edited by Edward Connery Lathem. Copyright 1939, © 1967, 1969 by Holt, Rinehart & Winston, Inc. Reprinted by permission of Henry Holt and Company, Inc.

Alfred A. Knopf, Inc. for "Dreams" from *The Dream Keeper and Other Poems* by Langston Hughes. Copyright 1942 by Alfred A. Knopf, Inc. and renewed 1970 by Arna Bontemps and George Houston Bass. Reprinted by permission of Alfred A. Knopf, Inc.

Little, Brown and Company, Inc. for "This Is My Rock" from *One at a Time* by David McCord. Copyright 1929 by David McCord. First appeared in *Saturday Review.* Used by permission of Little, Brown and Company, Inc.

William Morrow & Company, Inc. for eight lines from "Winter" in *Cotton Candy on a Rainy Day* by Nikki Giovanni. Copyright © 1978 by Nikki Giovanni; "A Snowflake Fell" from *It's Snowing! It's Snowing!* by Jack Prelutsky. Copyright © 1984 by Jack Prelutsky. By permission of Greenwillow Books (A Division of William Morrow & Company, Inc.). Both reprinted by permission of William Morrow & Company, Inc.

Marian Reiner for "Crickets" from *Crickets and Bullfrogs and Whispers of Thunder: Poems and Pictures* by Harry Behn, selected by Lee Bennett Hopkins. Copyright 1949, 1953, © 1956, 1957, 1966, 1968 by Harry Behn. Copyright renewed 1977 by Alice L. Behn. Copyright renewed 1981 by Alice Behn Goebel, Pamela Behn Adam, Prescott Behn and Peter Behn; "Whispers" from *Whispers and Other Poems* by Myra Cohn Livingston. Copyright 1958 by Myra Cohn Livingston; "A Lazy Thought" from *Jamboree: Rhymes for All Times.* by Eve Merriam. Copyright © 1962, 1964, 1966, 1973, 1984 by Eve Merriam. All rights reserved. All reprinted by permission of Marian Reiner for the authors.

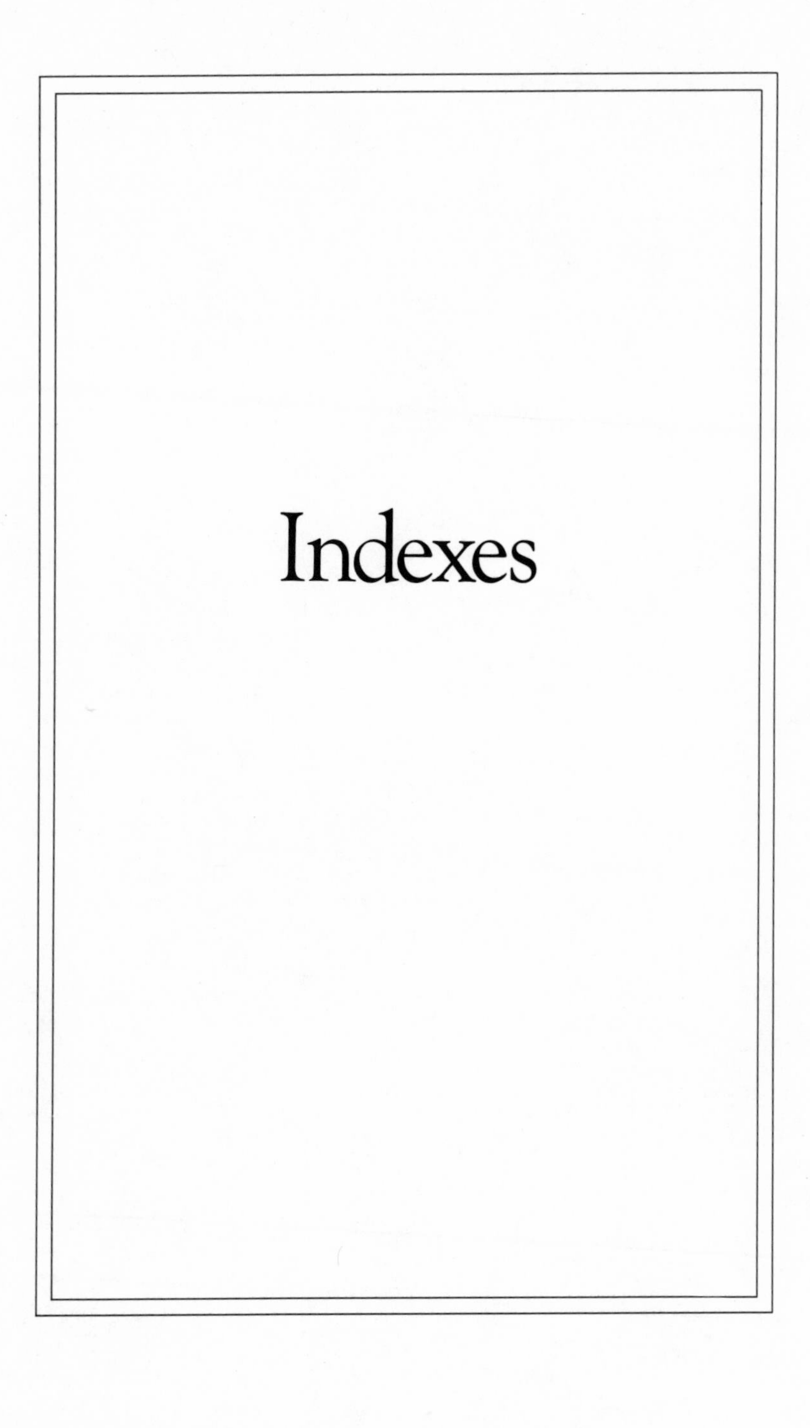

Indexes

Author Index

Adler, David, 185
Adoff, Arnold, 26–31, 146, 197, 200, 214
Aldis, Dorothy, 199
Armour, Richard, 197
Arnold, Matthew, 215

Baring-Gould, Cecil, 23
Baring-Gould, William, 23
Barnes, Joey, 144
Bates, G. E., 161–62
Bauer, Caroline Feller, 220
Behn, Harry, 32–36, 200, 203
Belting, Natalie M., 145
Benét, Rosemary, 192–93
Benét, Stephen Vincent, 192–93, 198
Berry, Faith, 81
Blackburn, George Meredith, III, 11
Blackburn, Lorraine A., 11, 159
Blake, William, 212–13
Bober, Natalie S., 71
Bodecker, N. M., 37–40, 200
Bontemps, Arna, 215
Bragdon, Carl, 152
Brewton, John E., 11, 159, 178
Brewton, Sara, 178
Brooks, Gwendolyn, 41–44, 54, 190, 200, 203, 205, 217
Browning, Elizabeth Barrett, 161
Browning, Robert, 157, 218

Carroll, Lewis, 160, 162–64, 178, 197, 212, 213, 218
Ciardi, John, 3, 8, 13, 45–51, 108, 145, 158, 178, 200, 215
Cleary, Beverly, 206
Clifton, Lucille, 52–55, 120, 200
Coatsworth, Elizabeth, 200
Cole, William, 195, 197, 215
Cooper, Kenneth, 213
Crapsey, Adelaide, 151–52, 179
Crofut, William, 213
Cummings, E. E., 9, 16, 178, 200, 213, 215

Dahl, Roald, 207
Davis, Ossie, 80, 81
de la Mare, Walter, 25
de Regniers, Beatrice Schenk, 56–60, 194, 196, 200, 230
Dickey, James, 215
Dickinson, Emily, 7, 200, 215

AUTHOR INDEX

Egita, Charles J., 181
Eliot, T. S., 4, 10, 12, 194, 217
Engvick, William, 212
Esbensen, Barbara Juster, 208

Fadiman, Clifton, 108
Farjeon, Eleanor, 18–19
Farley, Walter, 206
Field, Rachel, 179
Fisher, Aileen, 3, 61–67, 177, 190, 198, 200, 208
Froman, Robert, 165
Frost, Robert, 7, 14–15, 43, 68–72, 200, 203, 216, 217
Frye, Northrop, 216

Geisel, Theodor (Dr. Seuss), 24, 185, 200
Giovanni, Nikki, 73–77, 200
Greenfield, Eloise, 200

Henderson, Harold G., 148
Henry, Marguerite, 206
Hoffman, Herbert H., 216
Hoffman, Rita L., 216
Holmes, Oliver Wendell, 218
Hopkins, Lee Bennett, 10, 18, 32, 35, 82, 128–29, 178, 179, 180, 181, 191, 195, 197, 198, 202, 203, 205, 206, 207, 208, 209
Hubbell, Patricia, 206
Hughes, Langston, 7, 13, 78–84, 178, 180, 199, 200
Hughes, Ted, 120, 179

Jarrell, Randall, 213
Joubert, Joseph, 93

Kahn, Roger, 14
Keats, Ezra Jack, 205
Kennedy, Dorothy, 87, 141–42, 159, 161
Kennedy, X. J., 85–89, 141–42, 159, 161, 178, 200
Kilmer, Joyce, 198
Krauss, Ruth, 133
Kuskin, Karla, 3, 10–11, 90–94, 191, 192, 200, 203

Larrick, Nancy, 145, 192, 195, 205, 208, 212
Lathem, Edwin Connery, 69
Lear, Edward, 158, 159–60, 162, 200
Lewis, Richard, 147, 217
Lindsay, Vachel, 145
Livingston, Myra Cohn, 3, 14, 87, 95–102, 108, 135, 141, 153, 159–60, 161, 178, 179, 181, 190, 191, 198, 200, 203, 205, 206, 207, 208–9
Lobel, Arnold, 160
Longfellow, Henry Wadsworth, 54, 218

McCord, David, 3, 7–8, 18, 103–9, 153, 158, 162, 190, 197, 198, 200
McDonald, Gerald D., 7
McGinley, Phyllis, 162, 216
Meltzer, Milton, 80–81
Merriam, Eve, 3, 13, 110–15, 181, 190, 191, 193, 200, 205
Milne, A. A., 25, 200, 217, 229

Author Index

Moore, Lilian, 3, 116–20, 178, 200, 206
Moore, Vardine, 195
Morrison, Lillian, 214
Myers, Elisabeth P., 80

Nash, Ogden, 104, 198, 200
Nichols, Charles H., 81
Noyes, Alfred, 12, 13

Odland, Norine, 47
O'Neill, Mary, 188

Pellowski, Anne, 190
Plutarch, 216
Poe, Edgar Allan, 162
Prelutsky, Jack, 121–25, 179, 185, 195, 198, 200
Pritchard, William H., 71

Rampersad, Arnold, 81
Reeves, James, 179
Richards, Laura, 213
Ridlon, Marci, 177–78
Roethke, Theodore, 9, 178, 200
Roop, Peter, 35–36
Russo, Susan, 145, 209

Sandburg, Carl, 7, 9, 42, 112, 126–30, 178, 180–81, 199, 200, 202, 203, 216, 217
Sarkissian, Adele, 99
Sendak, Maurice, 133, 205, 212
Seuss, Dr. (Theodor Geisel), 24, 185, 200
Shakespeare, William, 12, 13, 145, 198, 200
Shattuck, Glen, 213
Shelley, Percy Bysshe, 216
Silverstein, Shel, 4, 131–35, 178, 182, 192, 198
Sims, Rudine, 53–54
Smith, William Jay, 200
Southey, Robert, 163
Starbird, Kaye, 197
Stevens, Wallace, 9
Stevenson, Robert Louis, 200, 213
Swensen, May, 120

Tennyson, Lord Alfred, 218
Thayer, Ernest Lawrence, 218
Thompson, Blanche Jennings, 217
Thurber, James, 212
Thurman, Judith, 120

Untermeyer, Louis, 15
Updike, John, 120

Viorst, Judith, 206–7

Walker, Alice, 80
Walter, Nina Willis, 144
Watts, Isaac, 162
Whitman, Walt, 54, 218
Wilder, Alec, 212
Willard, Nancy, 4, 200, 219
Williams, William Carlos, 8, 16–17, 162
Worth, Valerie, 200, 206
Wright, Richard, 146
Wyndham, Robert, 190

Zolotow, Charlotte, 133, 200

Title Index

Abraham Lincoln, 127, 128
"Against Idleness and Mischief," 162
"Age and Grade Expectancy in Poetry," 144
Alice's Adventures in Wonderland, 162–64, 213
"Alligator on the Escalator," 114
All Kinds of Time, 34
All Small, 105
All the Colors of the Race, 29
"All the world's a stage," 145
". . . And Then the Prince Knelt Down and Tried to Put the Glass Slipper on Cinderella's Foot," 206–7
And to Think That I Saw It on Mulberry Street, 24
Animals, Animals, Animals, 219
Animals in Verse, 219
Annie Allen, 42
Annotated Mother Goose, The, 23
"Archaeopteryx," 87
"Arithmetic," 18, 129
Arna Bontemps/Langston Hughes —Letters, 1925–1967, 81
Arnold Adoff Reads Four Complete Books, 29–30
As You Like It, 145
"Aunt Sue's Stories," 80, 81
"Away and Ago," 105

"Bam, Bam, Bam," 181
"Bananas and Cream," 197
Beat the Drum, Independence Day Has Come, 198
"Benjamin Bunnn," 192
"Best Part of Going Away Is Going Away from You, The," 49
Big Sister Tells Me That I Am Black, 29
"Bird of the Night," 213
Birds, 29
"Birthday," 198
Birthday Cow, The, 111
"Birthday Present," 177
Blackberry Ink, 113
Black Is Brown Is Tan, 26, 29
Black Judgement, 74, 75
Black Magic, 81
"Blow-up," 85
"Bobbing for Apples," 179
"Bogeyman, The," 179
Book of Americans, A, 192–93
Book of Pigericks, The, 160
"Boxes and Bags," 180–81

"Boy Named Sue, A," 134
Boy's Will, A, 69
Brats, 87
Break Dance Kids, The, 214
Bronzeville Boys and Girls, 41, 42–43, 202, 205
"Bubbles," 126
Bunch of Poems and Verses, A, 59

Cabbages Are Chasing the Rabbits, The, 29
"Calling All Cowboys," 50
Callooh! Callay!, 99, 198
Carl Sandburg Reading "Fog" and Other Poems, 130
Carl Sandburg's Poems for Children, 130
"Casey at the Bat," 218
Catch a Little Rhyme, 112, 114
"Catherine," 92–93
Cats, 4
Celebrations (Bauer), 220
Celebrations (Livingston), 99, 198
"Charge of the Light Brigade, The," 218
"Chicago," 128
Chicago Poems, 128
Chicken Soup with Rice, 205
Child as Poet, The, 99, 141
Chinese Mother Goose Rhymes, 190
"Chipmunk's Day, The," 213
Christmas Poems, 99, 198
Chrysalis, 35
"Cinderella," 207
Circle of Seasons, A, 99, 208
"Circles," 129
Circus, 123
Circus—A Teaching Unit, 185
"City," 13
Club, The, 111
Coffee-Pot Face, The, 62, 64
Cold Stars and Fireflies, 208
"Color," 82
Complete Poems of Carl Sandburg, The, 126, 127
"Construction Job," 181
Cornhuskers, 128
Cotton Candy on a Rainy Day, 73, 75–76
"Cradle Song," 213
Crate, The, 134
Crazy to Be Alive in Such a Strange World, 192
Creatures, 179
"Crickets," 32
Crickets and Bullfrogs and Whispers of Thunder, 32, 35
Cricket Songs, 34
"Crocodile," 87
"Crocodile, The," 213
"Cynthia in the Snow," 205

"Dangers of Taking Baths, The," 49
"Deacon's Masterpiece, The," 218
"Death of the Hired Man, The," 69–70
Did Adam Name the Vinegarroon?, 87
Dinosaurs, 206
Divine Songs Attempted in Easy Language, 162
Dogs & Dragons, Trees & Dreams, 90, 92, 94, 191, 192

Dog's Life, A, 195, 203
Don't You Turn Back, 82
Doodle Soup, 49
"Dracula Vine, The," 179
"Dragon of Death, The," 179
Dream Keeper and Other Poems, The, 81
"Dreams," 78, 81

Early Moon, 128
Earth Songs, 99
Easter Buds Are Springing, 198
Easter Poems, 99, 198
Eats, 29, 197
Ego-Tripping, 74–75
"Electric Eel," 87
"Eletelephony," 213
Everett Anderson's Goodbye, 52, 53
"Every Time I Climb a Tree," 105, 109

Far and Few, 104
"Father of a Boy Named Sue, The," 134
"Father William," 163, 213, 218
First Choice, 76, 94, 99, 109, 114
"Foghorns," 116
Forgetful Wishing Well, The, 85, 87
"For Mugs," 203
4-Way Stop, 98
"Frederick Douglass: 1817–1895," 82
Friend Dog, 29
Frost, 71
"Full of the Moon," 203
"Fury said to a," 164

"Gardener's Song, The," 218
Gathering of Great Poetry for Children, A, 217
Gemini, 75, 76
Generations, 53, 55
Giant Story, The, 58
"Gift Outright, The," 70
Giraffe and a Half, A, 133
Giving Tree, The, 133
Golden Hive, The, 35
"Golux's Song, The," 212
Good Dog Poems, 195
Good Morning, America, 9, 129
Good Morning to You, Valentine, 198
Gopher in the Garden, A, 122, 123
Go with the Poem, 120
"Grasshopper, The," 109
"Graveyard," 165

Haiku in English, 148
Hailstones and Halibut Bones, 188
"Hamsters," 177–78
"Haunted House, The," 179, 195
Have You Seen a Comet?, 190
Headless Horseman Rides Tonight, The, 123, 179
Hey-How for Halloween, 178, 198
"Hiawatha's Childhood," 218
Higgledy-Piggledy, 98
Highlights Book of Nursery Rhymes, The, 175

"Highwayman, The," 12
"Hokku Poems," 146
House at Pooh Corner, The, 229
"House That Jack Built, The," 161
"How Do I Love Thee?," 161
"How doth the little busy bee," 162
"How doth the little crocodile," 162–63
How Pleasant to Know Mr. Lear!, 99, 159–60
"Hughbert and the Glue," 90, 91, 192
Hurry, Hurry Mary Dear, 39
I Am the Cat, 10, 195
I Am the Darker Brother, 27
I Am the Running Girl, 29
Ice-Cream Ocean, The, 209
I Feel the Same Way, 117
If I Ran the Circus, 185
If I Were in Charge of the World and Other Worries, 207
"If We Walked on Our Hands," 59
"If You're Good," 183–84
"I Hear America Singing," 218
"I like it when it's mizzly . . . ," 205
I Met a Man, 48
In a Spring Garden, 146–47
"Incident of the French Camps," 218
Index to Poetry for Children and Young People, 11
"in Just-," 213
"In Memoriam to Langston Hughes," 83
International Index to Recorded Poetry, 216–17
Interviews with Robert Frost, 69
In the Clearing, 70
In the Witch's Kitchen, 178
Introduction to Poetry, An, 86
I Stood Upon a Mountain, 62
It Does Not Say Meow, 59
It Doesn't Always Have to Rhyme, 112
I Thought I Heard the City, 117
It's Christmas, 123, 198
It's Halloween, 123, 179, 198
It's Raining Said John Twaining, 39
It's Snowing! It's Snowing!, 121, 123
It's Thanksgiving, 123, 198
It's Valentine's Day, 123, 198
"I Woke Up This Morning," 93
"I wonder what the spring will shout . . .," 208

"Jabberwocky," 163, 213
Jamboree, 110, 112, 181, 191, 193, 205
"Jimmy Jet and His TV Set," 132
"John J. Plenty and Fiddler Dan," 50
Johnny Junk Is Dead, 30
"Juke Box Love Song," 82

"Keep a Poem in Your Pocket," 56, 196, 230

"Keziah," 42
"King Who Saved Himself from Being Saved, The," 50
Knock at a Star, 87, 141–42, 159, 161
"Knoxville, Tennessee," 75

Lady or the Tiger, The, 134
Lafcadio, the Lion Who Shot Back, 132–33
Langston, 80, 81
Langston Hughes (Berry), 81
Langston Hughes (Meltzer), 80, 81
Langston Hughes (Myers), 80
Langston Hughes (Walker), 80
"La Noche Triste," 69
"Lazy Thought, A," 110
Let's Marry Said the Cherry, 39
"Lewis Had a Trumpet," 92, 192
Life of Langston Hughes, The, 81
"Light in His Attic, The," 134
Light in the Attic, A, 4, 133, 134
Like Nothing at All, 62
"Likes and Looks of Letters, The," 18
Listen, Rabbit, 62
Little Hill, The, 34, 35
Little House of Your Own, A, 57
"Little Sounds," 59
Living Poetry, 218
Lollygag of Limericks, A, 98, 159
"Look Cinderella," 207
Lullabies and Night Songs, 212
"Madam" poems, 82
Mainly Mother Goose Songs and Rhymes for Merry Young Souls, 175
Make a Circle Keep Us In, 29
Malibu, The, 97, 98
Man Who Sang the Sillies, The, 49, 158
"Martin Luther King Day," 198
May I Bring a Friend?, 58–59
"Mean Song," 114
Meet the Newbery Author, 219
Merrily Comes Our Harvest In, 198
Mice Are Very Nice, 195
"Minotaur," 87
"Miracles," 219
"Mockingbird, The," 213
Moments, 208
Monkey Puzzle, 98
Monster Den, The, 49
Moon on the One Hand, The, 213
"Moon's the North Wind's Cooky, The" (Lindsay), 145
Moon's the North Wind's Cooky, The (Russo), 145
More Cricket Songs, 34
More Silver Pennies, 217
Mother Goose, 174
Mother Goose Book, The, 176
Mother Goose Treasury, The, 176
Mouse and the Motorcycle, The, 206
"Mummy Slept Late and Daddy Fixed Breakfast," 45–46, 49
Munching, 197

My Mane Catches the Wind, 195
My Parents Think I'm Sleeping, 123
"My Seed," 157

"Naming of Cats, The," 10, 11
"Negro Speaks of Rivers, The," 79, 82
"Never Bite a Married Woman on the Thigh," 134
"New Day," 37
New England Primer, The, 156
New Kid on the Block, The, 123
Night Before Christmas, The, 10–11
Nightmares, 123, 195
"Nikki-Rosa," 75
"Noise," 211
Nonsense Verse of Carroll and Lear, 160, 163
North of Boston, 69–70
No Way of Knowing, 98
Nude Descending from a Staircase, 86, 87
Nursery Rhymes, 175

"O Captain! My Captain!," 218
O Frabjous Day!, 99, 198
"Old Man's Comforts, The," 163
Old Possum's Book of Practical Cats, 4, 194
"Old Wife and the Ghost, The," 179
One at a Time, 18, 103, 104–5, 153, 158
One Little Room, an Everywhere, 99
One Winter Night in August, 87
O Sliver of Liver, 98, 153
"Otherwise," 63
Our Earth to Keep, 219
Out in the Dark and Daylight, 61, 66, 177, 208
"Out in the Dark and Daylight," 61
Out Loud, 112
OUTside/INside Poems, 29
Owlstone Crown, The, 87

Pack Rat's Day, The, 123
Panther and the Lash, The, 82
"Paper I," "Paper II," 129
"Passing by the Junkyard," 181
"Passover," 198
Pasture, The, 68
"Paulette," 42
"Paul Revere's Ride," 218
"Peanut Butter Sandwich," 182
"Pentagonia," 161–62
Person from Britain Whose Head Was the Shape of a Mitten, A, 39
Phantom Ice Cream Man, The, 87
Philharmonic Gets Dressed, The, 93
"Phizzog," 129, 202
Pick a Peck o' Poems, 218–19
Picture History of the Negro in America, A, 81
Pigeon Cubes, 37, 39

TITLE INDEX

Piping Down the Valleys Wild, 145, 195, 205, 208
"Pizza, The," 197
Pocketful of Poetry, A, 217
Poem Belongs to You, A, 219
Poems by Walt Whitman, 218
Poems for Glad, Poems for Sad, 217
Poems for Jewish Holidays, 99, 198
Poems for Christmas, 99, 198
Poems of Lewis Carroll, 218
Poems of Tennyson and Browning, 218
Poem Stew, 197
"Poetry," 18–19
Poetry and Reflections, 82
Poetry Explained by Karla Kuskin, 94
"Poetry for Children," 33
Poetry of Black America, The, 27, 146
Poetry of Horses, The, 195
Poetry of Langston Hughes, The, 82
Poetry of Robert Frost, The, 68
Poetry Parade, 36, 66, 94, 109
"Poetry Place," 142
"Poltergeist, The," 179
Prairie Town Boy, 128
Prelude: Selecting Poetry for Young People, 100
Prelude: Sharing Poetry with Children, 114
"Profile: Harry Behn," 35–36
"Profile: John Ciardi," 47
"Profile: Lucille Clifton," 53–54
Pursuit of Poetry, The, 15

"Question, The," 191

Rabbits, Rabbits, 66
Rainbows Are Made, 18, 128–29, 180, 202, 209
Rainbow Writing, 111
Random House Book of Poetry for Children, The, 123
Read-Aloud Rhymes for the Very Young, 123
Reason for the Pelican, The, 145
Reason I Like Chocolate, The, 76
Reckless Essay, 127–28
Report from Part One, 43
Restless Spirit, A, 71
Revolting Rhymes, 207
Ride a Purple Pelican, 123
"Riding," 182
"River Is a Piece of Sky, The," 145
Roar and More, 92
Robert Frost in Recital, 71
Robert Frost Reads "The Road Not Taken" and Other Poems, 71
Robert Frost's New England, 71
"Robert, Who Is a Stranger to Himself," 42, 202
Rootabaga Stories, 128

"Saint Patrick's Day," 198
Sandburg Treasury, The, 128
"Sarah Cynthia Sylvia Stout," 132, 192
Sea Is Calling Me, The, 209
"Search, The," 131
Sea Songs, 99, 208–9
Seasons of Poetry, 219

Seeing Things, 165
Selected Poems, 78, 180
"Seven Ages of Elfhood, The," 179
"Short Talk on Poetry," 128
"Show It at the Beach," 134
Shrieks at Midnight, 178
Sidewalk Racer, The, 214
Silver Pennies, 217
Sing a Song of Cities, 219
Sing Hey for Christmas Day, 198
"Skeleton Parade," 179
"Skipper," 41, 43
Sky Full of Poems, A, 112
Sky Is Full of Song, The, 207
Sky Songs, 99, 153
Smoke and Steel, 128
"Snowflake Fell, A," 121
Snowman Sniffles, 39
Snowy Day, The, 205
So Many Cats, 59, 194
"Some Cook!," 49
Some of the Days of Everett Anderson, 53
"Some Say the Sun Is a Golden Earring," 145
Something About the Author, 99
Something New Begins, 116, 119–20, 178
Something Sleeping in the Hall, 93
Something Special, 56, 57, 59, 196
Song in Stone, A, 181
Song I Sang to You, A, 95, 99, 181, 191, 205, 207
Song of Hiawatha, The, 218
Songs and Stories, 134
Songs from Alice, 213
Space Story, The, 93
Speak Roughly to Your Little Boy, 161–62
Speak Up, 105
"Spelling Bee," 18
Spin a Soft Black Song, 74
Sports Pages, 29, 214
Sprints and Distances, 214
Star in the Pail, The, 105
"Star in the Pail, The," 105
"Stopping by Woods on a Snowy Evening," 14–15
Surprises, 178, 191, 205
Swinger of Birches, A, 71

Take a Poetry Break, 220
Thanksgiving Poems, 99, 198
There Is No Rhyme for Silver, 112, 114
They've Discovered a Head in the Box for the Bread and Other Laughable Lyrics, 159
This Big Cat and Other Cats I've Known, 59, 194
"This Is My Rock," 103, 105
This Way to Books, 220
Through the Looking Glass, 162, 213
"Time for Building, A," 181
Today We Are Brother and Sister, 29
Tornado!, 29
To See the World Afresh, 120
"To the Dead in My Graveyard Underneath My Window," 152
Toucans Two and Other Poems, 123

Treasury of Nursery Rhymes, 175
"Turtle Soup," 197, 213

Under the Early Morning Trees, 29
"Unreasonable Excitement, An," 14

Vacation Time, 75
"Val," 42
Verse, 152
Visit from St. Nicholas, A, 10–11
"Visit to Robert Frost, A," 14
Visit to William Blake's Inn, A, 4, 219

"Walrus and the Carpenter, The," 218
"Warning, The," 179
"Waterfront Streets," 81, 180
Way of Knowing, A, 7
Way Things Are, The, 96, 98
Weary Blues, The, 80
"What Did You Put in Your Pocket?," 59
"What in the World?," 114
"What Is Gold?," 188
"What Is Orange?," 188
What Is Poetry?, 219
"What Is Red?," 188
"What Someone Said When He Was Spanked on the Day Before His Birthday," 50
"When I Heard the Learn'd Astronomer," 218
When It Comes to Bugs, 66
When It's Cold, and When It's Not, 219
Where the Sidewalk Ends, 131, 133, 134, 182, 192
"Whispers," 14, 95, 96
Whispers and Other Poems, 96
Why Am I Grown So Cold?, 179
"Why Pigs Cannot Write Poems," 49
Wind Song, 128
Windy Morning, 34, 35
"Windy Night," 213
"Winter," 73
Witness Tree, The, 70
Wizard in the Well, The, 35
Word or Two with You, A, 113
Worlds I Know, 98
Writing of Poetry, The, 100

"Yell for Yellow, A," 114
You Come Too, 71
You Know Who, John J. Plenty and Fiddler Dan, and Other Poems, 50
"You Mustn't Call It Hopsichord," 18
You Read to Me, I'll Read to You, 46, 49, 50
You Think It's Fun to Be a Clown!, 185

"Zombie, The," 179
Zoo Doings, 123

Index of Poets, Poems, and First Lines Appearing in Part Two

Adoff, Arnold, 26–31
"After a little bit of time," 52
"A snowflake fell into my hand," 121

Behn, Harry, 32–36
"black is brown is tan," 26
black is brown is tan, from, 26, 29
Blow-up, 85
Bodecker, N. M., 37–40
Brooks, Gwendolyn, 41–44
"Bubbles," 126

Ciardi, John, 45–51
Clifton, Lucille, 52–55
Crickets, 32

"Daddy fixed the breakfast," 45
de Regniers, Beatrice Schenk, 56–60
Dreams, 78

Everett Anderson's Goodbye, from, 52

Fisher, Aileen, 61–67
Foghorns, 116
"Frogs burrow the mud," 73
Frost, Robert, 68–72

Giovanni, Nikki, 73–77

"Hold fast to dreams," 78
Hughbert and the Glue, 90
"Hughbert had a jar of glue," 90
Hughes, Langston, 78–84

"I looked in the fish-glass," 41
"I'm going out to clean the pasture spring," 68
"I went to find the pot of gold," 131

Keep a Poem in Your Pocket, 56
"Keep a poem in your pocket," 56
Kennedy, X. J., 85–89
Kuskin, Karla, 90–94

Lazy Thought, A, 110
Livingston, Myra, 95–102

McCord, David, 103–109
Merriam, Eve, 110–15

INDEX OF POETS, POEMS, & FIRST LINES

Mummy Slept Late and Daddy Fixed Breakfast, 45–46
Moore, Lilian, 116–20
"Mornings bring," 37

New Day, 37

"Our cherry tree," 85
Out in the Dark and Daylight, 61
"Out in the dark and daylight," 61

Pasture, The, 68
Prelutsky, Jack, 121–25

Sandburg, Carl, 126–30
Search, The, 131
Skipper, 41, 43
Silverstein, Shel, 131–35
Snowflake Fell, A, 121

"The foghorns moaned," 116
"There go the grownups," 110
This Is My Rock, 103
"This is my rock," 103
"Two bubbles found they had rainbows on their curves," 126

"We cannot say that crickets sing," 32
Whispers, 95
"Whispers," 95
Winter, 73